GOD'S GIFT TO YOU

CHARLES SPURGEON

□□ Whitaker House

Unless otherwise indicated, all Scripture quotations are taken from the *King James Version* (KJV) of the Bible.

GOD'S GIFT TO YOU

ISBN: 0-88368-508-6
Printed in the United States of America
Copyright © 1997 by Whitaker House

Whitaker House
30 Hunt Valley Circle
New Kensington, PA 15068

Library of Congress Cataloging-in-Publication Data

Spurgeon, C. H. (Charles Haddon), 1834–1892.
    God's gift to you / by Charles Spurgeon.
      p. cm.
   ISBN 0-88368-508-6 (trade paper)
    1. Christian life—Baptist authors.   I. Title.
  BV4501.2.S714175   1997
  248.4—dc21   97-42134

3 4 5 6 7 8 9 10 11 12 13 / 09 08 07 06 05 04 03 02 01 00

Contents

Chapter 1

The Newness of Divine Mercy

*His compassions...are new every
morning: great is thy faithfulness.*
—Lamentations 3:22–23

Jeremiah's book of Lamentations is very heart-breaking. When you look at lonely animals in the desert, you have a fitting picture of his mournful state. His heart was ready to burst with sorrow and grief.

However, the prophet's whole tone changed when he called to mind the mercy of God. No sooner did he think of the compassion of the Most High than he at once took heart and began to sing as beautifully as David, the sweet singer of Israel. Truly, if we would only reflect on our mercies instead of focusing on our troubles, we would also exchange our mournful tunes for songs of joy.

It is true that God's people are a tried people, but it is equally true that their grace is equal to their trials. *"Through much tribulation* [they] *enter into the kingdom"* (Acts 14:22), but they do enter, and

7

the thought of the coming kingdom sustains them in their present tribulation. They wade through the waters of woe, often chest high, but the waves do not, and will not, drown them. They are still able to sing, even in the midst of the storm.

I would suggest to any who are in the habit of complaining—a very bad habit—to any who have become chronic murmurers, that this state of mind is sinful. On the other hand, remembering God's mercy and gratefully talking about it is a virtuous habit, one that honors God, as well as strengthens and profits our own souls. Imitate Jeremiah, then; if you can find no comfort in your present outward circumstances, meditate on the unfailing mercies of God.

What a blessed word the prophet used—*"compassions"*! The psalmist David used the word *pity* more frequently than the word *compassion,* but he meant the same thing. *Pity* is a humbling word, though extremely comforting. I have often felt very deeply chastened in my own soul by that text, *"Like as a father pitieth his children, so the LORD pitieth them that fear him"* (Ps. 103:13). What! Is this the Lord's attitude toward the strongest and the best of saints? Does God only pity them? Yes, it is true. Those who do heroic deeds, those who lead God's army in the day of battle, those whom we look up to with respect and admiration, God looks upon with infinite love, but that love still takes the form of pity. He can see their weaknesses where we see their strengths. He can discover their defects where we admire the work of the Holy Spirit in them, and He regards them with pity. Yet, it is a father's pity, a father who smiles at the weakness of the child, knowing that the feeble attempt the child is making will educate him for something better. The pitying father foresees that the child will ultimately outgrow his weakness and be able to do greater things.

God has compassion on His people, but it is compassion prompted by love. It is not the pity that is akin to scorn, but the pity that melts from love, just as honey drips from the honeycomb. Dear reader, if you are tried and troubled, think of the infinite pity of God toward you. He has struck you, but still not as hard as He might have done; out of pity He has held back His hand. He has spoken sharply in your conscience, but if He had spoken as loudly as your sins deserve, there would have been thunderclaps instead of admonitions.

Perhaps, as with Jonah, God has withered your gourd (Jonah 4:6–11). However, if He had done what justice might have demanded, it would not have been the gourd that withered, but you yourself! Admire the compassion of God! If one of your children is sick, at least they are not all sick. If He has taken away one of your friends by death, at least He has not taken away all your friends. If you have had heavy financial losses, at least you are not bankrupt. If you are sick, at least you have not been attacked by the diseases that have attacked some others; at least your pain is bearable. If the weather is dull and heavy to your spirit, at least it is not quite the blackness of the valley of the shadow of death. Take heart, even in the midst of trials, for the compassion of God is still to be seen.

Moved by such thoughts as these, the prophet penned the remarkable words before us: *"His compassions...are new every morning: great is thy faithfulness."*

I have been admiring the first part of the text, which suggests to me the newness of divine mercy. As you read this chapter, I want you to wake up your recollections, to turn over a few pages in your old journal, and to remember what God has done for you since you have known His name.

God's Mercies Are Always Novelties

God's mercies are *"new every morning."* Water that is in a pitcher may last for a long time, but it will not remain fresh. It might have been fresh the first morning that I filled the pitcher, but it will not be fresh the next day. The longer it lasts, the more stagnant it becomes. But the water from a well-spring is always new. I can drink of it when I am a boy, go to it in the prime of manhood, and stoop to drink of it when my hair turns gray. It is always new and sparkling.

God is not the pitcher, but the fountain. Our treasures that we lay up on earth are stagnant pools, but the treasure that God providentially and graciously gives us from heaven is the crystal fountain that wells up from the eternal deeps and is always fresh and new. There are no gray hairs on the angel of mercy, no wrinkles on his brow. I may say of him what the sweet writer said of the spouse: *"His locks are bushy, and black as a raven"* (Song 5:11). Mercy is of old and is forever God's beloved attribute, yet it is always bright, fair, clear, and young. Mercy is not a tree that yields its fruit only once a year, making it necessary to store the fruit through the depths of winter and to preserve it until, perhaps, it becomes rotten. On the contrary, mercy is the Tree of Life, which bears its fruit every month (Rev. 22:2). At all times and at all seasons we may receive the compassion of God, and we will find that it is *"new every morning."*

The thought that God's mercy is always new is a pleasing one, but that it is *"new every morning"* is very wonderful. If you had to preach, you would find it difficult to have something new to say every Sunday, but God has something new for us every morning. I suppose the columnists in our newspapers often have to search their brains to give us something new, but God, with the greatest of ease, sends to His millions of people something *"new every morning."* He does not need to repeat Himself. If He sends the same mercy, there is still something new about it that makes it fresh. God never gives us old mercy that is worn-out; His mercy always comes fresh from the mint, with all the gloss and all the brightness of new coins. *"His compassions...are new every morning"*— not some mornings, but every morning, from the first of January to the last of December. God never has to pause to think of something fresh, but His mercies come to us freely, spontaneously—*"new every morning."* Let us explore this subject further.

Because the Morning Ends the Night

In the first place, every morning brings a new mercy because every morning ends the night. The night is the hour of danger and dismay. Why do we ask concerning the sick, "Did he make it through the night?" We do not ask, "Did he make it through the day?" Is it not because, somehow or other, we have connected the night with the idea of insecurity and danger? We wear the image of death when we sleep; how slight the difference is between how a sleeping man looks and how a dead man looks.

Every morning we may say, "What a mercy that my bed did not become my tomb! What a mercy that, in the night, I was not alarmed by a fire! What a mercy that my bed was not burned up with me on it! What a mercy that my house was not broken into by

11

burglars! What a mercy that no tornado or earthquake terrified me! What a mercy that no cry of anguish, like the shrieks that woke up every parent in Egypt, was heard in my house because my child was dying!" Such cries have been heard by some of us, and we have had dreadful nights that we will never forget for as long as we live. But every morning in which we wake, whether such terrors have just occurred or whether we have had a sweet, quiet night, we have a new mercy. Every morning we may at once look to the text and say, "Another night is gone, and Your mercies are *new every morning.*"

Because the Morning Ushers In a New Day

Every morning also brings a new mercy because every morning ushers in another day. That is a new call to praise, for we have no right to an hour, much less a day.

To the sinner, it is a great mercy to have another day of grace, another opportunity for repentance, a little more time in which to escape from hell and fly to heaven, a new reprieve from death. Ah, soul, suppose that you had never seen the light of another rising sun, but had heard instead the dreadful sentence, "Depart, cursed one, into the darkness that will never be pierced by a ray of light!" What a mercy that you have been spared!

The Christian may thank God that he has another day in which he may walk with God as Enoch did; another day in which he may trust God as Abraham did; another day in which he may work for Christ as Paul did. He has another day in which he may reap the gospel harvest; in which he may gather pearls for Emmanuel's crown; in which he may ripen for glory; in which he may commune with the Lord; in which he may make advances in the divine pilgrimage toward the heavenly city. God gives us our days; may He teach us their value, for they are priceless pearls. Then, when the morning breaks, we may truly say, "Your mercies are fresh every morning, for the morning has brought us another day."

Because the Morning Brings Fresh Supplies

Furthermore, a new mercy comes to most of us in that each morning brings supplies for the day. I have often thought to myself, "What a mercy to know that when I wake there will be breakfast for me!" There are many, sad to say, who do not know where the first meal in the day will come from. That is a sorrowful thing, and a very heavy discipline, but it is certainly not the case with most of us. There is enough in the cupboard for the next day. When we rise in the morning, we are not quite like the sparrows, who have to seek their food. However, even though they have no food yet, they sing as soon as they wake. There is nothing in their barn, so to speak, but they sing. Martin Luther heard them and wrote,

> Mortal, cease from care and sorrow;
> God provideth for the morrow!

After singing, the sparrows set to work to find their daily bread, and find it they do, for God feeds the birds of heaven.

Now, your day's provision is waiting for you. As with the Israelites, there is the manna outside the camp for you, and you know where to gather it. As you bless the name of the Lord, remember His mercy.

But you do not have all that you wish, you say, and so you are not happy. Ah, remember the apostle

13

Paul's words: *"Having food and raiment let us be therewith content"* (1 Tim. 6:8). Learn the apostle Paul's lesson:

> *I have learned, in whatsoever state I am, therewith to be content. I know both how to be abased, and I know how to abound: every where and in all things I am instructed both to be full and to be hungry, both to abound and to suffer need.* *(Phil. 4:11–12)*

I am afraid that some of my readers—especially those who have abundance—do not keep in mind that they are daily dependent on God's providence. Let me remind you that you receive your daily bread from God as much as if the ravens were to bring it, as they did for Elijah (1 Kings 17:4–6). You obtain all that you receive from the hand of God as certainly as if it were to drop from the clouds, or as certainly as if the winds were to bring you quails (Num. 11:31). Be thankful, then, that as each day brings your household its need for daily bread and clothing and shelter, God is pleased to meet your needs by giving you His mercies every morning.

Because We Sin Every Morning

In spiritual things, my fellow believer, how richly the text may be illustrated. God's *"compassions...are new every morning"* because every morning I commit new sins. Strange creature that I am, I can scarcely open my eyes to the light before my soul begins to display its darkness! Miserable human that I am by nature, I can scarcely breathe without offending God by the thoughts and imaginations of my heart. Even though I may guard my eyes, mind my tongue, and keep the members of my body pure, still my heart wanders and my tongue speaks idle words before long! But, fortunately, new pardon always comes. God's *"compassions...are new every morning,"* and so we wash once again and are clean. We go to the

> Fountain filled with blood
> Drawn from Emmanuel's veins.

When we go to our jobs, and strain and strive, we are prone to wander from God. Yet we may think of our Master, who wrapped a towel around Himself, took a basin, washed His disciples' feet, and then said that they were completely clean. Our daily pollutions need a daily cleansing. We have been washed once in the blood, making us clean before God. But we need to be purged daily from our defilements, and every morning brings us this grace.

Because the Morning Brings New Temptations

We scarcely leave our bedroom, no, we do not even leave it, before the morning brings new temptations. Some mornings bring us temptations that we have never experienced before. Suggestions gain entrance into our own minds that never perplexed us until that moment. We scarcely know what to do with them, and young Christians, especially, are staggered when these diabolical arrows are shot toward them. Then, when we leave our homes, who knows how long it will be before we will be sorely tempted to sin? Ah, if we only knew when the thief were coming, we could watch out for him. Satan and sin come unexpectedly like a thief in the night.

The time when the child of God is most likely to sin is when he is in the holiest frame of mind. You may think that is an odd remark, but I make it from experience. I have often found that when I have been nearest to God in prayer, or when I have most enjoyed a service, I have then been met by somebody who has said something cross, wicked, or unkind. I have been tempted to answer, and perhaps have answered, in an ungodly way. After having your mind lifted up, you are not exactly prepared for these contrary people. Just when you are in a moment of the highest joy, something may trip you up.

Well, now, it is such a mercy to think that when I begin the morning, though I cannot know what temptations may come, I can know that God's mercies are *"new every morning."* Therefore, there will be fresh grace to sustain me through the fresh temptations. We see this in 1 Corinthians:

> *There hath no temptation taken you but such as is common to man: but God is faithful, who will not suffer you to be tempted above that ye are able; but will with the temptation also make a way to escape.* (1 Cor. 10:13)

Put on the gospel armor. Then let the arrows fall where they may, for they will not wound you. Even if a wound is received between the joints of the armor, there is a tree whose leaves are *"for the healing of the nations"* (Rev. 22:2). A heavenly hand will deliver these leaves so that the wounds may be healed. Let us be glad, then, that there is daily grace for daily conflict.

Because the Morning Brings New Duties

My fellow believer, we do not know completely when we wake what the particular tasks of the day will be. Each new morning brings new duties. Even if we did know completely what was appointed for the day, it would be a sad thing to wake up to new responsibilities and new duties if we did not also have new strength. Every day brings a new duty, or it may be an old duty in another shape and cast in another mold. All that I did yesterday cannot exonerate me if I am idle today, and all the service that I did for my Master a year ago will be no excuse if I waste this year. I must take each hour of time as it flies by and seek all the wealth that can be found in it.

Beloved, there will be daily strength given to you for the daily duty to which God calls you. You can be sure that if God has us work for Him, He will not have us go to war at our own expense, but He will provide His soldiers with weapons. He will provide the worker in the vineyard with tools. There is daily grace, then, for new duties.

I might go on to mention that each day will bring its trials. Each day will bring its anxieties and necessities, but each morning brings us the promise, *"As thy days, so shall thy strength be"* (Deut. 33:25). Note that the word *days* is plural. Many say, "As thy day," but the verse reads, *"As thy days."* As long as days last, until days are all swallowed up in time and time is swallowed up in eternity, God's compassions will be *"new every morning."* His new compassions will meet our new needs, our new relationships, our new responsibilities, our new temptations, and our new sins.

I will try to illustrate this subject in another light, for this text is very much like a kaleidoscope. You may turn it as many times as you want, and there is constantly a fresh form of beauty to be seen.

Some Mercies Are New in Themselves

Sometimes the mercies we receive are actually new in themselves. I am sure that you have had times in life when a new mercy has been bestowed upon you. Perhaps you have set up a monument in your mind, as Jacob set up a pillar at Bethel, to commemorate some particular favor that has made a certain day memorable. Such mercies as these have been particularly new.

Sometimes the mercy is new in substance—you receive what you never received before. At other times the mercy is not so much new in substance as it is new in the way that it comes. Yesterday, after having prayed for the last two or three months that God would remember the various works I am involved in, I received a thousand pounds for the Stockwell Orphanage from an unknown donor. I certainly felt that this was a new mercy. Money has been sent for the work at different times, but it has always been sent in a different way or a different form. Each time it has nearly overwhelmed me.

When I heard about the anonymous donation yesterday, I was sitting with a dear brother who had just been saying to me, "My dear friend, there are some people who say, 'Our friend Spurgeon does not know where to stop; he is always going on from one good thing to another. If he should fail, it would be a very dreadful thing.' Now, don't you think it would be a great catastrophe? What a great deal of money is required for the college, for instance." Then he went on to mention other financial needs. "Suppose the needed funds should fail to come in!" he said, to which I replied, "I never suppose any such thing. I have no purpose to serve and no end to gain, and no motive but God's glory. I was forced into these works against my will, and God cannot leave me. He must

18

carry on the work, and I am persuaded that He will. My motto is 'Jehovah Jireh.'"

At that moment the mail came, and I opened the letter that contained the thousand pounds. My friend just said, "My dear brother, let us kneel down and pray," and so we did. With many tears we thanked God earnestly from the heart. I then knew how foolish we were to talk about things failing that are undertaken for God, because God is sure to help us. My friend said that the donation was a blessed means of grace to him. He said he would remember that day as one of the best days of his life because God had shown him that He will help those who undertake work in His name for the poor and needy and who try to aid His cause. Well now, was that not new? It was not a new thing for us to receive help, but it came in a new way. God's mercies are *new every morning.*"

Sometimes, when you do not get the mercy in exactly a new way, it seems new to you because you are in a new condition. You have more knowledge and can better comprehend the value of the mercy. You have more experience and can better understand your own need of the mercy.

I am sure that the light in which an aged man regards a mercy, is a different light, in some respects, than that in which a young man regards it. The babe in grace is very grateful and sees that the mercy is precious, but the man in Christ Jesus has a gratitude of a richer kind. The mercy is new because we see it in a new light, and it finds us in another state.

The mercy that comes to a young man of twenty has a brightness about it; the mercy that comes to the same man at seventy may not have as much sparkle, but if the man is a mature Christian, I think that he will have a deeper and more solemn sense of obligation. As we grow in life, the glitter of our

19

thoughts may depart, but the solid gold of them will increase and multiply if we really mature in spirit as well as age in years. Unfortunately, growth in grace is not always synonymous with growth in years. May the Lord grant that we grow in Him!

How Should We Respond?

Since God's mercies are *"new every morning,"* what should our response be?

New Praise

First, I call upon you for new praise. I ask, in the name of Jesus Christ, whose new mercies you and I are always receiving, that our hearts praise Him hour by hour. Weave new crowns for Christ! Sing new songs in honor of His blessed person and in honor of the mercy that flows to us from Him.

No, I do not ask merely for words of praise, but also for acts of praise, which will speak louder than words. Do not be content with what you have done. Out of gratitude, do something new, if possible. As the soldier who marches forward, let us do something more advanced. Let us be even like the eagle that soars to the skies, circling higher and higher, or like the wind that gathers its strength and blows stronger and stronger. May God grant that we do not rely on our past accomplishments, saying, "We did this when we were young," or, "We gave that yesterday." But, as the new mercy comes, let there be on our part new acts of service.

New Faith

And I ask not only for these new actions, but also for new faith. Let every mercy confirm our confidence in the God of mercy. All these compassions of our covenant God are ready witnesses against our unbelief. All these loving-kindnesses are reliable evidences to confirm our confidence in God. "At what time," God may say to us, "have I been false to you? Have I been a wilderness to the church? Have I received you for a season and then cast you away? Have I been slack in blessing you? Have I been sparing with My mercy? Have I withheld My loving-kindness?" You do not dare to say that God has been stingy toward you. His mercies have been *"new every morning."*

Since God has given so bountifully to us, we should give back to Him. Surely you do not want God to have to say to you,

> *Thou hast bought me no sweet cane with money, neither hast thou filled me with the fat of thy sacrifices: but thou hast made me to serve with thy sins, thou hast wearied me with thine iniquities.*   *(Isa. 43:24)*

Oh, may He not need to scold us in this way, but let our reasoning be, "What can I give to the Lord for all His blessings to me?" (Ps. 116:12). Let us give Him new praise, new thanksgiving, and new acts of gratitude.

New Prayers

I ask, then, for new confidence in God. Perhaps you cannot mount as high as this. At any rate, I ask every reader who has known the faithfulness of God to offer Him new prayers. If your prayers have already been answered, pray again. The beggar in the street says, "Help me this time, and I'll never ask again." Oh, you who beg at mercy's door, do not say that. Rather,

From His mercy draw a plea,
And ask Him still for more.

God's promise is, *"Open thy mouth wide, and I will
fill it"* (Ps. 81:10). Go to God, and expect Him to ex-
ceed your faith and do for you *"exceeding abundantly
above all that* [you] *ask or think"* (Eph. 3:20).

My fellow Christian, exercise a holy ingenuity in
inventing new plans for the honor of Christ. Exercise holy perseverance in carrying out those plans.
Fan the flames of your holy zeal every morning in
order to carry out those plans fervently and earnestly. Even as His loving-kindnesses are *"new every
morning,"* may our grateful contemplations be new
every morning.

Great Is Your Faithfulness

God's faithfulness is so great that there has
never been an exception to it. He has never at any
time acted toward any one of His people other than
according to truth and righteousness. It is a marvelous thing when a man is very honest and very upright. Yet, if he runs an extensive business, it will be
very difficult for him to be free from charges of
wrongdoing. He may be completely innocent, but
still it will be very difficult for him to remain free
from accusations, especially if he has many employees. But our God has had millions of people to deal
with throughout all ages, yet there is not a single
soul on earth who can say that God has ever failed to
deal with him in faithfulness.

But, more than that, God has never failed to
keep all His promises. At a ripe old age, Joshua said,
*"Not one thing hath failed of all the good things
which the LORD your God spake concerning you"*

(Josh. 23:14). If a person makes many promises, it is difficult for him to keep them all. Even if he has the ability to keep them, he will not always be able to remember them. But God remembers every promise that He ever made, and He is careful to honor each of those promises in the experiences of those who believe in Him. Those who trust in God will find Him to be good not only in great things, but also in little things. He keeps the oath of His covenant forever. His faintest word will abide, and the least truth that He has ever declared will never grow dim. He is a tree whose leaves will not wither; He brings forth His fruit in His season (Ps. 1:3).

The glory of God's faithfulness is that no sin of man has ever made Him unfaithful. Unbelief is a most damning thing, yet, *"if we believe not...he abideth faithful"* (2 Tim. 2:13). When His children rebel against His law and wander far from His statutes, He will discipline them, yet He says, *"My lovingkindness will I not utterly take from him, nor suffer my faithfulness to fail"* (Ps. 89:33). God's saints may provoke the Most High, yet He will have compassion on them and turn to them and say, *"I, even I, am he that blotteth out thy transgressions for mine own sake, and will not remember thy sins"* (Isa. 43:25). No sin of man can make God unfaithful.

In addition, no emergency that can possibly arise can ever compel God to be unfaithful to His people. If the whole world should lie in ruins, He will still bear up the pillars of His people's hope. When His saints can no longer be safe under heaven, He will take them up to heaven. When He commands the tongues of fire to consume this world, when the elements are dissolved with intense heat, if we *"are alive and remain"* at the coming of the Son of Man, we will be *"caught up together...to meet the Lord in the air"* (1 Thess. 4:17).

God always provides an ark for Noah before He sends the flood. He always has a mountain ready for Lot before He destroys Sodom. If David must be driven from the king's court, he will be housed in Engedi. If the Philistines come against the land, God will be sure to raise up His servant to deliver His people from the enemy. In each crisis, God will be there. You can be sure that He has not forgotten you. When the clock strikes and the bell tolls the hour, God will arise for the defense of His people and will show Himself strong on behalf of all those who trust in Him.

Settle it in your minds, beloved, that He cannot lie. Believe every man to be a liar, if you will, but never believe that God can fail you. Perhaps, deep down inside, you are saying something like this: "Sometimes I see the wicked prosper while I am in tribulation and distress, and my spirit says, 'Has God forgotten? Will He give all the good things to those who curse Him? Will He cause His people to be chastened forever?'"

If you are saying that, say it softly, and then add, "Although this is the way things seem, I know that *God is good to Israel, even to such as are of a clean heart'* (Ps. 73:1). *'Though he slay me, yet will I trust in him'* (Job 13:15). *'The LORD gave, and the LORD hath taken away; blessed be the name of the LORD'* (Job 1:21). *'It is the LORD: let him do what seemeth him good'* (1 Sam. 3:18). *'In quietness and in confidence shall be your strength'* (Isa. 30:15). *'Trust in the LORD, and do good; so shalt thou dwell in the land, and verily thou shalt be fed'* (Ps. 37:3)." Hold on to your faith as the Grecian warrior held on to his shield. Your safety depends on it. *"Cast not away therefore your confidence, which hath great recompense of reward"* (Heb. 10:35). When you cannot rejoice in the light of His countenance, trust in the shadow of His wings. Like David, you will learn to rejoice even there.

Fellow Christian, I hope that you will meditate on this subject in times to come, and I ask God to awaken in you a life of holy joy and confidence.

If you are a non-Christian, how I wish that you knew something about the experiences of God's people! You who have a worldly mind-set and have no faith in God know little about the joys of Christians. Although I have written extensively about the sorrows of God's people, the joys of faith are unspeakable. One drop of God's love would sweeten a sea of bitterness. I will even go so far as to say that even the pangs of hell would lose their bitterness if one drop of Christ's love could flow there and be tasted by those who are lost.

But if you are a Christian, you already know what it means to find roses among thorns. You have found your pains and sufferings to be soul-enriching things, messengers sent by the King to take you to His banquet and to lead you to discover hidden treasures. You know this. Tell it to the ungodly, and perhaps their mouths will start watering for the good things on Christ's table. Once they long for them, they will have them, for Christ never refuses a hungry one. And if there is such a one reading this book—a poor, empty, destitute soul—remember, mercy's door always stands open, and Christ, the owner of the Gospel Inn, always stands ready to receive every soul who comes. He has written this over the door of the inn: *"Him that cometh to me I will in no wise cast out"* (John 6:37).

Chapter 2

The Tenderness of God's Comfort

As one whom his mother comforteth, so will I comfort you; and ye shall be comforted in Jerusalem.
—Isaiah 66:13

I have never hesitated to assert my conviction that there are great blessings in store for God's ancient Israel. The day will come when her comfort will abound, when the glory of the Gentiles will flow to her like a stream, when she will be comforted by her God *"as one whom his mother comforteth."* But I believe that our text applies to all the servants of God. This comforting verse of Scripture is theirs, whether Jew or Gentile, slave or free, male or female. We *"are all one in Christ Jesus"* (Gal. 3:28). All the promises are ours in Him, for in Him all the promises are *"yea"* and *"Amen"* (2 Cor. 1:20). I believe, then, that this passage belongs to every child of God.

It is reassuring that there is such a promise as this on record, for believers need comfort. They need comfort because they are men, and *"man is born unto trouble, as the sparks fly upward"* (Job 5:7).

Man has had a great need for consolation ever since he was expelled from Eden. Unfortunately, believers are not exempt from this need for comfort. Although favored by God, elected by His sovereignty, and called by His grace into a state of acceptance, believers are still encumbered by the body, and they keenly feel this disadvantage. They are tempted in all ways as other men are, and in some ways even more so. They are men, and only men, at best.

Another reason that Christians need comfort is the fact that they are God's children, for if others escape God's correction, God's children must not and will not. The Lord may be pleased to give the sinner a long prosperity so that he may be fattened as a sheep for the slaughter, but His promise to His people whom He calls by His grace is, *"You only have I known of all the families of the earth: therefore I will punish you for all your iniquities"* (Amos 3:2). *"Whom the Lord loveth he chasteneth, and scourgeth every son whom he receiveth"* (Heb. 12:6). Therefore, we certainly need special consolation, since, as men—as mere men and as Christian men—we have a constant need for comfort.

When I present a text like this, I know there are many readers who feel that it does not apply to them; but, my dear reader, if you are a Christian, it will not be long before it does. You will look back, perhaps, at the words that I write in this chapter and say of them, "God sent them to me as a preparation before the trial came. He gave me food as He did Elijah under the juniper tree, because He determined that I should go forty days in the strength of that food." Do not despise the consolations of the Lord because you do not need them just now. You will require them later on. The calm will not last forever; a storm is brewing. Do not say, "My mountain stands

27

firm; I will never be moved." God only has to hide His face, and you will be troubled (Ps. 30:7). Then you will prize what you lightly esteem now. You will long to be comforted *"as one whom his mother comforteth."*

I think I may very well explain our text in three parts: first, who it is that comforts; second, how He comforts; and, third, where He comforts.

God Comforts Us

Who is it that comforts us in our trials? Who is the "I" in this verse: *"As one whom his mother comforteth, so will I comfort you"*? We find that it is God.

The work of comforting His saints is not too lowly for God to be engaged in. It is true that He uses instruments, but all real comfort for a broken heart must come directly from God Himself. He does not say, "I will send an angel to comfort you," but, *"I* [will] *comfort you."* Nowhere in the text does it say that the Christian minister will comfort you. Unfortunately, we who preach the Word are often nothing but *"broken cisterns, that can hold no water"* (Jer. 2:13). But our text says, *"I* [will] *comfort you."* When God undertakes the work, then the minister becomes a conduit that is full even to bursting with the drink that the hurting Christian requires. Then the thirsty soul can be satisfied even out of poor earthen vessels like ministers. But it must be God's work; He must do it. When a soul is truly humbled and heavily burdened and broken in pieces by God's hand, there is only one hand—the pierced hand—that can heal the wound.

As the Trinity

When we read in this passage that God will comfort the soul, I think we are to understand that He

28

does so in the trinity of His person. He is called *"the God of all comfort"* (2 Cor. 1:3), and He first comforts us as our Father. The very use of that term *father* seems to bring comfort to many hearts. As long as I can say "my Father," I will not be without a star in my sky. "My Father"—that sweetens all the sorrow that can come to me. I may be pierced by a sword, but, my Father, it is in Your hands. I may have to drink from a bitter cup, but, my Father, You have given it to me, and will I not drink it? The term *my Father* will make my heart leap for joy in the midst of my deepest distress. As a father, God actively comes to the comfort of His children. When a childlike spirit is put within us, our souls will lean on His all-sufficient grace and will rejoice even in the midst of deep distress.

God the Son also comforts us, for is His name not *"the consolation of Israel"* (Luke 2:25)? When you stand at the foot of the cross, you see comfort there for all the evils that pain your heart. Sin loses its heaviness; death itself is dead; all griefs expire, slain by the griefs of the Man of Sorrows. Only enter into the Savior's passion, and your own suffering is over. Get to understand His sorrows, and your sorrows find at least a pause, if not an end.

As for the blessed Spirit, He was given for this very purpose—to be our Comforter. He dwells in all the saints to bring to their remembrance the things that Jesus spoke (John 14:26), and to lead them into all truth (John 16:13) so that their joy in Christ may be full.

It is something very delightful to consider that the Father, Son, and Spirit all cooperate to give us comfort. I can understand their cooperating to make the world; I can understand their cooperating to save a soul; but I am astonished at this same united action in so comparatively small a matter as the comfort of believers. Yet the Holy Three seem to think it a great matter that believers should be happy, or they would not work together to cheer sorrowful spirits. *"I* [will] *comfort you,"* says our Lord.

In Various Ways

We must understand that when God says, *"I* [will] *comfort you,"* there are various ways by which He does so. Sometimes He comforts us in the course of providence. We may be the lowest spoke of the wheel right now, but as time rolls on, we may be the highest. We may suffer acute pain tonight, but by morning the Master may have eased all our pain. The pause between sickness and health may not be very long. If the Good Physician puts His healing hand on us, we will soon be restored.

How often, when you thought you were coming to your worst, has there been a sudden brightening of the sky? It is a long lane that has no bend, and it is a long trouble that never comes to a close. It is when the sea ebbs as far as it can go that the tide begins to flow, and it is said that the darkest part of the night is just before daybreak. When the winter grows bitterly cold, we begin to hope that spring will come soon. Likewise, when our desperate sorrows reach their worst, they are coming to a close. Therefore, let us take heart. The sea will not always be so rough, poor troubled saint. You will be in peaceful waters before long. Before many years have rolled by, you will be out of the seas altogether and standing on the solid ground of eternal joy.

However, when the Lord is not pleased to comfort us through the means of providence, He has a means of doing it by His omnipotent, secret working on the human heart. Have you not found that sometimes, when you were very burdened with trouble, a very special calm came over your spirit? You had been distressed and were almost in a frenzy, but when you woke one morning, you felt calm and peaceful. You had given up rebellion, left off murmuring, and you could sing these words:

> Sweet to be passive in Thine hands
> And know no will but Thine!

Have you not been conscious, even in times of severest trouble, of an unusual joy? You did not sing with your voice, but there was something within you that sang softly, silently, but still sweetly. You sometimes look back upon that sickbed—I know I do—and almost wish that you were there now. The trial was sharp indeed:

> Sharp are the pangs that nature gives.

But, oh, the joy that came with them! It was so surpassing that in retrospect you forget the pain and only remember the sweetness. How did this happen? Did the pain accomplish it? Nothing of the kind. God is like a watchmaker who knows how to touch the wheels of the watch and regulate them because he made the watch. He made us; therefore, He knows how to deal with us so that everything will go right, whereas everything went wrong before.

He can open the floodgates of joy and inundate our souls with bliss, even in our darkest days of trouble. "Only hope in Me, My child," He says, "for you will yet praise Me. I am your help and your God." *"Although the fig tree* [does] *not blossom"*

31

(Hab. 3:17), although your income is reduced and fire destroys your earthly possessions, your God can make up for all this. He can cause your days of leanness to be days of fatness, and your days of hunger to be days of feasting, and your days of thirst to be days of drinking.

With Previous Provisions

It would not be fitting to close this point without remarking that God has been pleased to store up provisions for the comfort of all His saints. When He comforts, He does not have to create something new to do it; He only has to bring to us provisions that have been laid up—fruits new and old that have been made ready for His beloved.

If trouble comes, God has provided a strength by which you will meet it or a way through which you will escape it. There are promises in God's Word suitable for every conceivable condition of God's people. Concerning the millions of His people living in different countries and under different forms of government and in different ages, all of them with different temperaments and constitutions, their trials take all kinds of shapes. As a kaleidoscope shows an endless variety of patterns, there is an infinite variety of tribulations undergone by God's people. Yet, for every single case that has arisen, there has always been a promise that—word for word and letter for letter—has met the case.

In the big bunch of keys in that good old Book, there is a key for every lock. Even if it were not so, there are one or two promises like master keys that will fit all. Such a promise is the following: *"Fear thou not; for I am with thee: be not dismayed; for I am thy God"* (Isa. 41:10). This promise will suit the youth and the elderly; it will be satisfactory to you if you have to overcome difficulties or if you have to endure sufferings. In the calm or in the battle, lying in the trench or climbing the ladder, that text will still be precious. *"Fear thou not; for I am with thee: be not dismayed; for I am thy God."* Let us fall back, then, on the comforting truth that God will console His children. He Himself is responsible for their comfort, having promised to be their Helper. Therefore, we may gain nourishment from our text: *"As one whom his mother comforteth, so will I comfort you."*

How Does He Comfort Us?

We have learned that it is God who comforts, but how does He comfort? As a *"mother comforteth."* This is an especially delightful metaphor. A father can comfort, but I think he does not feel at home doing so. When God speaks about pity, He selects the father: *"Like as a father pitieth his children"* (Ps. 103:13). But when He speaks about comfort, He selects the mother.

When I have seen my little ones sick, I have felt all the pity in the world for them, but I have not known how to comfort them. But a mother knows by instinct how to do it. There is placed in the mother's tender heart a power of sympathy, and very soon she finds the word or gives the touch that will meet her darling's situation and cheer his troubled soul. The father is awkward at it. His rougher, sterner nature is hardly skilled in the matter of consolation, but the mother can do it to perfection. It is good, therefore, that the text selects the mother, but there are other reasons besides. How, then, does the mother comfort her child?

First, she does it very fondly. Some, when they care for a patient, stand back and tell him, "There is the medicine, if you would like to take it." But the mother's way of doing it is to gently hold the spoonful of medicine to the child's lips—to hold the child close while she gives it. She does not talk to him at arm's length, but she holds him to her heart all the while. That is probably the secret of her power.

And so, when God comforts any poor burdened sinner or troubled saint, He does not talk to him at a distance. He runs and throws His arms around him and kisses him. The infinite, almighty God throws His arms around a repenting sinner and gives him the kiss of His love. He does just the same to a troubled and afflicted saint. He comforts fondly.

Should we dare apply such a word as *fondly* to the great God? Should we say that He has a fondness for His children? Yes. In fact, if there is a word more sweet or more dear, indicating a closer affinity and a deeper and purer love, we may use that word concerning our God. He loves us with a love that has no bottom, no summit, and no shore. Even as He loves His own dear Son, so He loves us. We are in His heart; we are engraved on the palms of His hands (Isa. 49:16). Therefore, when He comforts, it is in so fond a manner that we cannot help but be cheered. All the tenderness that a mother has, God has for us. He comforts us as a mother comforts her child.

With Sympathy

However, there is more than fondness here. A mother comforts her child with much sympathy. She always seems to feel the pain that the child is feeling. To soothe that headache, she lays her cool hand upon the hot, throbbing little brow. She herself is pained as she thinks of the pain that must be there. Or, she looks at the hand that is bleeding because of a fall, and her eyes brim with tears for the little one. She feels it all; therefore, she is sure to comfort well. This is how Jesus comforts.

I once heard of a little child who said to her mother, "Mother, Mrs. Smith, the widow, says she likes me to visit her, for I comfort her so well. When she sits and cries, I put my head in her lap and I cry, too, and she says that comforts her." Ah, yes, child, there is truth in that. This is just the sort of comfort we need, and this is just what God does. Our Lord in human flesh still sorrows with His people. He hungers in their hunger, thirsts in their thirst, and mourns in their mourning. Even though He reigns on high, He is not so high that He has no *"respect unto the lowly"* (Ps. 138:6).

Tirelessly

Also, a mother comforts her child tirelessly. She is not satisfied with saying half a dozen words and putting her child down. She picks him up, and if he will not be bounced on one knee, she tries the other. If that form of comfort will not do, she will try another. I heard of a good mother who wanted to teach her child a particular thing. When people complained that she had to repeat the same thing twenty times, she answered, "Yes, I did that because nineteen times would not do." In the same way, God perseveres.

Sometimes a mother may have to comfort her child when he is very sick and fretful and his poor little head and heart are troubled. She has to comfort him again and again and again. The soft words are always on her lips. She can do nothing else but just console the little one, and she does not grow tired of it.

Oh, these mothers of ours! They never do grow tired when their children are sick. They seem to be up all night and all day long. If a nurse comes for a few hours, they are up even then, looking after the nurse. Our mothers are so untiringly kind. Well, I say to you who have fled to Jesus for refuge, that our God is kinder than any mother. His Book is full of attempts to comfort His children, and those attempts—blessed be God—are not without success.

Seasonably

Again, a mother comforts her child seasonably. A true mother does not comfort her child all the time. If she is a silly mother, she brings up her child so delicately that he turns out to be a viper that bites her. If she is a wise mother, she saves her comforts until they are needed. When the child is sick, then she gives the medicine.

Well, God does not comfort His saints all the time. When they are in affliction, then He consoles them. As our tribulations abound, so our consolations abound by Jesus Christ (2 Cor. 1:5). A balance is kept. If there is an ounce of trouble, there will be an ounce of comfort; if there is a ton of trouble, there will be a ton of comfort.

When the child has been doing wrong and the parent has disciplined him, if he sticks out his little lip, if he lies down and kicks and screams, the wise mother does not comfort him. But when the child comes and asks to be forgiven, the mother's heart is ready to forgive immediately. "Sin no more," she says, "and the past will be forgiven and forgotten." Well, this is how God comforts us. While we are proud and stand against Him, we will feel His correcting hand; but when we confess our faults and come humbly to Him for pardon, we will have seasonable comfort, *as one whom his mother comforteth.*"

Effectively

A mother's comfort also has this aspect to it: she usually comforts in a most effective manner, and the child goes away smiling. Though he seemed to say before, "I will never be happy again," five minutes of a mother's wise talk and sweet comfort makes the child as happy as before. "Ah," you say, "that will do for children, but it will not do for men." But God keeps His saints like children before Him. May God grant us to be like little children; otherwise, we cannot enter the kingdom of heaven (Mark 10:15)! When our God comforts us, I am quite sure He does so more effectively than the tenderest mother.

Always

A mother comforts all her life. "A mother is a mother all her life," says an old proverb. There is no change there. *"Can a woman forget her sucking child, that she should not have compassion on the son of her womb?"* (Isa. 49:15). It seems impossible. Even if it is possible, *"Yet,"* says God, *"I* [will] *not forget thee"* (v. 15). A mother does not cast away her child. Fathers sometimes have done such things, but mothers, I should hope, never. But even if they have, the Lord remains faithful.

Should nature change
And mothers monsters prove,
Zion still dwells upon the heart
Of everlasting love.

God will not cease to comfort His people. Perhaps you are passing through a very severe trial, and you think you will never be comforted again. Well, dear believer, your mother will not forsake you, and do you think God will? "But," someone says, "you do not know my difficulty; it is a crushing one." My dear friend, I know I do not know it, but your heavenly Father knows. If an earthly mother sticks by her child, do you suppose that He will leave you? Go to Him. His heart is as fond toward you now as when you were on the mountain rejoicing in the full sunshine of His love. He never changes in the least. Go to Him with confidence and humble faith, and you will find the text true: *"As one whom his mother comforteth, so will I comfort you."*

Where Does He Comfort Us?

We have answered the first two questions: Does God comfort? and, How does God comfort? The third question is, Where does God comfort? The text says, *"In Jerusalem."*

In the Place of Trouble

Jerusalem was the place where God's ancient people had their troubles. The city was besieged. Oh, people of Jerusalem, how you were made to weep! What sorrow rolled over you, to see the city dismantled and her palaces become ruins, to see wild fowls and animals inhabiting the place where once the assembled tribes were glad! Oh, Jerusalem, what grief your name causes to your former inhabitants as they remember you. The glory has departed, and the sorrow lasts still! Yes, but God will comfort His people in the very place of their trouble. This will be fulfilled on a large scale in the millennial glory. Then our world, which has been the scene of the saints' sorrow, will also be the scene of their triumphant reign with Christ Jesus.

Meanwhile, you, His servant, must not suppose that because you have trials you are in the wrong place. The vine is not in the wrong place simply because the vinedresser often uses the knife; it may be the best place for that vine. Beware, young people especially, of self-will in seeking to change your troubles. You may think that because you are single you have exceptional troubles. Do not be in a hurry to incur the troubles of married life! You who are lowly employees think that you are treated harshly. Do not be in such a hurry to be a supervisor. I sometimes find that my cross is not exactly what I would like it to be, but I would be very much afraid to attempt to alter it. It is better and wiser to bear the problems we have than fly to others that we know nothing about. The man whom you envy would probably be the object of your pity if you knew more about him.

Be content to stop in Jerusalem. Remember, the comfort that God gives will be a comfort to suit your present place and position. Even *"in Jerusalem,"* where you have seen the furnace of God placed, for His *"fire is in Zion, and his furnace in Jerusalem"* (Isa. 31:9), you will have your comfort. It is a joy to think of Daniel in the lions' den. I believe that Daniel never had a sweeter night's rest than when he

had some old lion for his pillow and the younger lions for his guardians. And in the case of Shadrach,
Meshach, and Abednego, the Master did not break
down the furnace walls and take them out at once,
but He was with them in the fire and cheered them
in the midst of the flames. Likewise, the comfort of
God will come to you in your time of need.

Allow me to present another view of this: God
will comfort you who are here below. Some people
say, *"Oh that I had wings like a dove!"* (Ps. 55:6).
Now, what would you do if you had them? They
would be very awkward equipment for a man, but
suppose you had the wings of a dove. What would
you do? Would you fly away? Well, you would hardly
dare to do that, for to fly to God without permission
would be taking the matter into your own hands.
Can God not comfort you where you are?

"Ah," some people say, "I expect to have my
happiness in another world." So do I, but I hope to
have some here, too. "One heaven will be enough for
me," some people say. But why not have heaven here
and heaven hereafter, too?

> The men of grace have found
>   Glory begun below.
> Celestial fruits on earthly ground
>   From faith and hope may grow.
> Then let our songs abound,
>   And every tear be dry.
> We're marching through Emmanuel's ground
>   To fairer worlds on high.

It is true that the fairer worlds are on high, but it is
equally true that we are on Emmanuel's land even
now. *"In Jerusalem"*—the place of your trials—*"will
I comfort you."*

And now, to come to another meaning of the passage, *"in Jerusalem"* can mean "in the church of God." The richest comforts are reserved for those who, fearing the Lord, speak to other believers often and are not ashamed to acknowledge His name (Mal. 3:16). And I think, dear friend, the place of comfort is the assembly of God's people. Therefore, do not forsake *"the assembling of* [y]*ourselves together, as the manner of some is"* (Heb. 10:25).

There are people in the world who never go out to a weeknight church service—never think of such a thing. They sit in an easy chair after the day's work; there they sit and say, "Well, my soul is full of doubts and fears. I cannot rejoice as I used to do."

> What peaceful hours I once enjoyed!
> How sweet their memory still!

Now, those people expect God to come to their house and comfort them. Why should they expect any such thing when they refuse to go to God's house for comfort? Our Lord will sometimes withhold a sense of His presence from us in order to make us feel our wrongdoing in staying away from the means that He has appointed for our comfort and consolation.

You can ignore what I have just said about church attendance if you are faithful in attending church, even on weeknights. What I have said will be to you like one pastor's sermon about those who go to sleep in church. When he finished it, he realized he had done no good, for, as he said, "Only those who were awake heard it!"

Rather, I would recommend to you faithful ones that, whenever you meet a friend who is greatly in need of comfort and is complaining that he has not gotten any, you give as tactful a hint as you can that he may lack the comfort because he neglects the means of grace. He who will not go to the store and buy cannot be surprised if he does not have any food for supper. He who will not take the trouble to go to the well must not complain if he suffers thirst. Oh, let us, dear friends, as often as we can, gather together with the Lord's people in praise and prayer. No doubt, *"in Jerusalem"* we will find our comfort.

There are some people who talk about their enjoyments in God's house, and it does one good just to listen to them! There are some who say to the Lord about His house, "Master, it does us good to come here, and we thank You, Lord, that You make the place of Your feet glorious (Isa. 60:13). We long for Sunday to come around again, for we feel that the church is an oasis." In their case, God always makes His house to be a fountain of living waters to their souls.

To that end, I ask the Master to help all His servants! Pray for your ministers, but remember that the comfort cannot come from them. It may come through them, but it must come from the Master Himself. With that exhortation, I remind you of the gracious promise of our text: *"As one whom his mother comforteth, so will I comfort you; and ye shall be comforted in Jerusalem."*

May God add His blessing and cause troubled sinners to look to Christ, and Christ will have the glory!

Chapter 3

Comfort for Despondency

Thou knowest not what a day may bring forth.
                              —Proverbs 27:1

What a great mercy it is that we do not know *"what a day may bring forth"*! We are often thankful for knowledge, but in this case we may be particularly grateful for ignorance. *"It is the glory of God to conceal a thing"* (Prov. 25:2), and it is most certainly for the happiness of mankind that He conceals their future.

Suppose that bright times were predicted for us in the book of destiny and we could read that book now. We would probably squander our days until the bright times arrived. We would have no heart for the present. If, on the other hand, we knew that there were dark days of trouble in store for us, if we knew exactly when they would come, probably the thought of them would overshadow the present. The joys that we now drink would be left untasted because of our nervous fears about the distant future. To know the good might lead us to presumption; to know the evil might tempt us to despair.

Fortunately, our eyes cannot penetrate the thick veil that God hangs between us and tomorrow. We cannot see beyond the spot where we are now, and, in a certain sense, we are utterly ignorant about the details of the future. We may, indeed, be thankful for our ignorance.

However, although we do not know *"what a day may bring forth,"* although we cannot see into the immediate future, we can be thankful that we do know something about the far-reaching future. We differ from the animals in this respect. When, two or three nights during the week on my way home, I pass a flock of sheep, or a little herd of cows, all going down to the butcher's, traveling in the cold, bright moonlight toward the slaughterhouse, I feel thankful that they do not know where they are going. What misery they would suffer if they knew anything about death. The lamb's thoughts are in the fold, and it is completely unaware of the slaughterhouse. It licks the hand that is about to kill it, not knowing of its coming speedy death. It is the happiness of the beast not to know the future.

However, in our case, we know that we must die, and if it were not for the hope of the resurrection and the hereafter, this knowledge would distinguish us from the animals only by giving us greater misery. God must have intended for us to live in a future state, or else He would have benevolently left us ignorant of the fact of death. If He had not meant for our souls to begin to prepare for another and a better existence, He would have kept us ignorant even of the fact that this existence will pass away. But, having given us an intellect and a mind, which know from both observation and inward consciousness that death will come, He wants us to prepare for what will follow death.

We do know the future in its great rough outlines. We know that, if the Lord does not return first, we will die. We also know that our souls will live forever in happiness or in sin. According to whether we are found in Christ or without Christ, our eternal portion will be one of ceaseless bliss or never ending agony. We should be thankful that we know this so that we can be prepared for eternity. However, to return to my original thought, we should also be thankful that we do not know the future in its details, that it is shut out from our eyes lest it should have an evil influence on our lives.

Solomon addressed the words of our text to the boasters, the people who say, "*'To morrow we will go into such a city...and buy and sell, and get gain'* (James 4:13). Then, when we have amassed much wealth, we will say, *'Soul, thou hast much goods laid up for many years; take thine ease, eat, drink, and be merry'* (Luke 12:19)." Solomon seemed to put his hand on the boasting man's shoulder and say, "You fool! You do not know what you are saying. You do not know what will happen tomorrow. Your goods may never come to you, or you may not be here to trade with those goods at all. You build a castle in the air, but you think your fantasies are true. You are like someone who dreams about a feast and wakes to find himself hungry! How can you be so foolish?" Solomon pondered our text very solemnly and said, *"Boast not thyself of to morrow; for thou knowest not what a day may bring forth"* (Prov. 27:1).

Solomon used this text to shame our growing pride and our certainty of prosperity. I do not intend, however, to use the text with this objective. Instead, I will use it to encourage those who tend to be gloomy. I want to shed a ray of light into the thick darkness of their fear.

Those Fearing the Future

Our text will comfort those who are fearing and trembling concerning some evil that is yet to come.

My friend, you are afraid. You cannot enjoy anything you have because of this terrible and fearful shadow that has fallen across your path—the shadow of an evil that you say is coming tomorrow or in a couple of months or even in six months. Now, you are not quite certain that this evil will come, for you do not know what may happen tomorrow. You are as alarmed and afraid as if you were quite certain that it would happen. But it is not certain. *"Thou knowest not what a day may bring forth."* Since it is uncertain whether it will happen or not, had you not better leave your sorrow until it is certain? Meanwhile, leave the uncertain matter in the hand of God, whose divine purposes will be seen to be wise and good in the end. At the very least, small as the comfort may be, there is still comfort in the fact that you do not know what may happen tomorrow.

Let me just expand this thought a little for those of you who are fearing tomorrow. We very often fear what will never occur. I think that the majority of our troubles are not those that God sends us, but those that we invent for ourselves. As the poet speaks of some who "feel a thousand deaths in fearing one," so there are many who feel a thousand troubles in fearing one trouble, which, perhaps, will never have any existence except in the workshop of their own foggy minds.

It is a harmful task for a child to whip himself. It might be good for him to feel the whip from his father's hand, but it is of little benefit when the child applies it himself. Yet, very often the strokes that we dread never come from God's hand at all but are purely the inventions of our own imaginations and our own unbelief working together. There are more people who howl under the lash of unbelief than who weep under the gentle rod of God.

Now, why should you fill your pillow with thorns grown in your own garden? Why are you so busy gathering nettles with which to strew your own bed? There are enough clouds without your thinking that every little atom of mist will surely bring a storm. There are enough difficulties on the road to heaven without your picking up stones to throw into your own path to make your road rougher than it ever needed to be. You do not know what may happen tomorrow. Your fears are absurd. Perhaps your friends know that they are absurd, but certainly you ought to know so, too. Do you not know that God can utterly avert the trouble you are dreading? Perhaps tomorrow morning you will receive a letter that will entirely change the face of the matter. A friend may intervene where you least expected, or difficulties that were like mountains may be cast into the depths of the sea. *"Thou knowest not what a day may bring forth,"* and the trouble that you dread so much may never occur at all.

Moreover, do you not know that even if the trouble should come, God has a way of overruling it? Even you, poor trembler, will stand by and see the salvation of God and will be amazed at two things— your own unbelief and God's faithfulness. You say that the sea is before you, that the mountains are on either side, and that the foe is behind you, but you do not know what will happen tomorrow. Your God will lead you through the depths of the sea and put a song in your mouth that you never could have known if there had been no sea, no Pharaoh, and no mountains to shut you in. These trials of yours will be the winepress out of which you will receive the wine of consolation. This furnace will rob you of nothing but your dross, which you will be glad to get rid of. Your pure gold will not be diminished by so much as an ounce but will only be the purer after it all. The trouble, then, may not come to you at all, or if it comes, it may be overruled.

There is one more thing. If the trial does come, your God has promised that *"as thy days, so shall thy strength be"* (Deut. 33:25). Has He not said many times in His Word that He *"will never leave thee, nor forsake thee"* (Heb. 13:5)? He never did promise you freedom from trouble; He speaks of rivers and of your going through them. He speaks of fires and of your passing through them, but He has added,

> *When thou passest through the waters, I will be with thee; and through the rivers, they shall not overflow thee: when thou walkest through the fire, thou shalt not be burned; neither shall the flame kindle upon thee.*   (Isa. 43:2)

What does it matter to you, then, whether there are fires or not, if you are not burned? What does it matter to you whether there are floods or not, if you are not drowned? As long as you escape with spiritual life and health, as long as you come out of all your trials the better for them, you may rejoice in tribulations. Thank God when your temptations abound. Be glad when He puts you into the furnace, because you are sure to receive a blessing from the experience.

So then, since you do not know what may happen tomorrow, take heart, you fearing one, and put your fears away. Do as you have been instructed. *"Delight thyself also in the LORD; and he shall give*

48

thee the desires of thine heart" (Ps. 37:4). *"Cast thy burden upon the LORD, and he shall sustain thee: he shall never suffer the righteous to be moved"* (Ps. 55:22). Did David not say, speaking by the Holy Spirit, *"Many are the afflictions of the righteous: but the LORD delivereth him out of them all"* (Ps. 34:19)? I charge you, therefore, to be of good cheer, since you do not know what may happen tomorrow. That is my word to fearful saints.

Those in Present Trial

Now I will address the text to another group of Christians, whose painful position really deserves more pity than that of those who only invent their fears or are troubled about the future. I mean those who are troubled at the present moment because of distress and affliction.

We little know, fellow believer, how many cases of distress may be present all around us. Truly the poor have not disappeared out of the land. We *"have the poor always with* [us]" (Matt. 26:11). Furthermore, some of the poor need other mouths to speak for them, since from their very independence of spirit and their Christian character they are slow to speak for themselves. There may be a trouble in my neighbor's heart that is almost bursting it, while I stand peacefully by. We should *"remember them that are in bonds, as bound with them"* (Heb. 13:3). We should sympathize with those who are troubled as if we ourselves were troubled.

It will not be a waste of time, then, if I say to you who are troubled about earthly concerns, that there is comfort for you in this passage. *"Thou knowest not what a day may bring forth."* You say, "It is all over for me; I will give up in despair." No, friend, wait at least one more day before you give up, for you do not know what could happen in a day's time. If tomorrow does not bring you deliverance, keep hoping for one more day, at least, for you do not know what tomorrow could bring. And I would keep on going with the same attitude until the last day of life. At least for one day more there is no room for despair. You cannot conclude that God has forsaken you or that providence has utterly turned against you. You do not know what may happen tomorrow, so wait until you have seen that day out. Do not give yourself up as a hopeless victim to despair until you have seen what tomorrow may bring you.

What unexpected turns of events there have been in the lives of those who have trusted in God. If you are trusting in yourself, you may help yourself as best you can; but if you are trusting in God, you have ample reason to expect that God will come to your assistance. You must watch and work as if everything depended on you, but you must also remember that everything does not depend on you.

Sometimes God has intervened so wondrously to help His servants at what we call "the nick of time," that they have hardly been able to believe their own senses. "Strange!" they say. "It is like a miracle." Indeed, it is, for the difference between the old dispensation and the new is that God used to work His wonders by suspending the laws of nature, whereas now He does greater things than this. He achieves His purposes quite as marvelously and lets the laws of nature remain as they are. He does not make the ravens bring His people bread and meat, but He gives them their bread and their meat somehow. If I may say so, using ravens is a clumsy method, but it is a more divine method to use the common things of this life to achieve the same end.

Nowadays, God does not make the manna fall from heaven. No doubt some people would like Him to do so. Even so, He brings the manna. He provides food and clothing, with which every Christian should be content (1 Tim. 6:8). He supplies His people's needs by ordinary means, and in this He is to be wondered at and adored. Look up, then. Wipe away that tear. Do not for a moment consider murmuring against God. Do not go home to your wife and children with that sorry tale and tell them that God is not faithful to you! Wait until tomorrow, at any rate, for *"thou knowest not what a day may bring forth."*

And to you who are troubled about spiritual things, I might quote the same text. You say, "Ah, I have been hearing the Word for a long time, and all that I have gotten from it is conviction of sin, and hardly even that! Oh, how I wish that God would bless the Word to my soul! I am longing to be saved! What I would give to be a Christian, a true and sincere Christian, one in whom the Spirit of God has put a new heart and a right spirit!" You say, "Oh, I have sought salvation by listening to the Word, and I have sought it through earnest prayer. However, months have passed, and I have made no progress. I have no more hope now than I had long ago. I seem as far away from the attainment of eternal life as I was when I first heard the Word. No, if possible, I am even further away. The Word has been a *'savour of death unto death'* to me, and not a *'savour of life unto life'* (2 Cor. 2:16)."

Well, my dear friend, do not give up listening to the Word. Do not give up going to the Lord's house, for if you have received no blessing up to this point, yet, since you are going in the right direction, the Lord may meet with you, for you do not know what may happen tomorrow.

How many years those poor people waited around the pool of Bethesda, expecting that an angel would, at a certain time, come and trouble the water (John 5:2–4)! There they waited. Although they were disappointed dozens of times by others stepping in first, they continued to wait because it was their only hope.

Now, it is by using the proper means that you are likely to get a blessing. *"Faith cometh by hearing, and hearing by the word of God"* (Rom. 10:17). Do not, therefore, be persuaded to cease hearing, for you do not know what may happen tomorrow. The very next sermon you hear may be the means of your enlightenment. The very next testimony at the prayer meeting may give you encouragement. The very next time the gospel trumpet sounds, you may find your liberty, and what a blessing that liberty will be! When you do find it, you will say it was well worth waiting for!

Let me add another word: do not give up praying. It is a common device of Satan to say to the soul, "The Lord will never hear you; you are one of the reprobate. He has never written your name in the Book of Life." Soul, pray as long as you have breath. Let it be your firm resolution to remain at the throne of grace. Say to yourself,

> If I perish I will pray,
> And perish only there.

It is not said that the gate of mercy will open to the first knock. If it did, there would be no room for the virtue of perseverance. But the Lord, who delights in our persistence, encourages us with the promise that one day the gate will be opened. *"Ask, and it shall be given you; seek, and ye shall find; knock, and it shall be opened unto you"* (Matt. 7:7).

And who knows how soon this may be! Why, before you close your eyes tonight, you may be able to look to Christ crucified and find peace. Instead of the weeping prayer at the bedside, there may be a happy prayer of another kind, not with tears of sorrow, but with tears of holy joy, to think that the Lord has enlightened your darkness, that you have looked unto Christ and now your face is not ashamed. Why not? Why should it not be tonight? Why should it not be tomorrow? May God grant, poor downcast one, that it be so.

At any rate, let me repeat the advice I have already given. Since you cannot know that God will not hear you; since it was never revealed to any man, and never will be, that God will not regard his cry; if you can get no further than the question of the king of Nineveh, still go on. Nineveh's king asked, "'Who can tell' (Jonah 3:9) what may be?" Likewise, "thou knowest not what a day may bring forth."

I will tell you one thing, and you may take it as being God's own truth: if you go to Christ empty-handed, guilty, and willing to take all your salvation from Him as a free gift, and if you cast yourself upon Him, the day will bring forth eternal life to you—salvation, joy, and peace. It will bring forth adoption, for you will be received into the divine family. It will bring forth to you the foretaste of the heaven that God has prepared for His people. You will know a blessed day here that will be a foretaste of a never ending day hereafter, a day that will be as one of the days of heaven upon earth.

I wish that the Lord would bless these words of mine to those of my readers who are despondent. You may be sustained for a while and helped up by what I have said. But, better still, if you will now be filled with a desperate resolve to cast yourself at the foot of the cross, then little do you know what the day will bring forth! You cannot imagine the joy you will have or the peace you will receive. The pardon that Christ will give you is far richer than you have thought it could be, and the success with which your prayers will be crowned is far more marvelous than even your best hopes have conceived. *"Thou knowest not what a day may bring forth."*

Those Who Have Worked Unsuccessfully

Now, thirdly, turning this time not to those who are fearing the future or to those who are disconsolate about present affliction, I would like to address a few words to those who are worn-out in the Master's service.

I can scarcely sympathize, as I wish to do, with those who have worked for Christ unsuccessfully. I have never had to say, "Master, I have fished all night and caught nothing"; therefore, I can only speak about what I suppose to be the feelings of unsuccessful men. For many years I have been preaching the Gospel, and I do not know that God has blessed me more at any time than He is blessing me now. Nor can I say that at any time He has ever blessed me less, for it seems as if He has always given me more than I can receive and has blessed the Word exceeding abundantly above what I have asked or even thought (Eph. 3:20). In my situation, there is room for nothing but gratitude, encouragement, humble dependence on God for the future, and adoring joy for the past and the present.

However, what hard work it must be for a minister or a Sunday school teacher to go on preaching and laboring without any success, or with so little that it is only like a cluster here and there upon the highest bough. I can imagine such brothers and sisters feeling that they can speak no more in the name of the Lord. However, as they weep over their failure and say as Isaiah said, *"Who hath believed our report? and to whom is the arm of the LORD revealed?"* (Isa. 53:1), I would not be surprised if my text should whisper in their ears a comforting thought: *"Thou knowest not what a day may bring forth."*

Do not stop laboring, dear believer! You are fainting today, but tomorrow you may rise with new strength. You may feel as if you are nothing but weakness itself in the morning, but, though you may hardly know how it came about, in the evening you may be happy and cheerful. The divine presence may overshadow your heart and drive your fears away, consoling you in your distress and reassuring you that it is good to be God's servant, even if one were to have no present reward.

And after this, what if you should find yourself, next time you do your work, discharging it with an unusual zest and with a sacred power? What if the pulpit, instead of being a prison as it has been to you, suddenly becomes a palace? What if, instead of feeling like a mere bush in the wilderness, God should dwell in the bush and make you all ablaze, like that unconsumed fire that Moses saw? What if the stammering tongue should suddenly be unloosed, and the cold heart should suddenly be all aglow with divine enthusiasm? What if the poor tongue of clay should suddenly become a tongue of fire? What a change it would be! *"Thou knowest not what a day may bring forth."* You never can tell!

And what if, while you yourself are awakened in this way, there falls a similar awakening on the people—on the children in your class or the hearers in the house of prayer? What if, instead of the dull, leaden eyes, which look as if death itself were gazing out from them; what if, instead of stony and motionless hearers, there should suddenly be a holy sensitivity given to the people? What would you say to that? Yet, why should there not be? Sometimes such grace comes all at once.

The rock is struck repeatedly—for a long time it will not break—but, suddenly, there comes a blow of the hammer that is, perhaps, not as hard as many blows before it, but hits the stone in the right place, and the stone breaks to pieces. "Oh," you say, "I could keep on doing my work if I thought that this would happen." Keep on doing your work, then, believer, for you do not know what will happen next. Pray for great things, and you may then expect them. You may not be sure of such blessing if you have not prayed for it, but, after you have sought it, why should it not come? Therefore, keep doing the work.

I believe all Sunday school teachers find that sometimes a sudden softening comes over their classes. Similarly, ministers often realize that all of a sudden, they scarcely know how, there is a noticeable change in their hearers, so that preaching becomes a totally different experience. I am very conscious of the difference between the various congregations I address. Almost every day, and sometimes twice a day, I am preaching. Occasionally, it is dreadful misery because, say what I will, I know it is not a sympathizing audience. I feel as though I were a plow dragging over the rough ground. But, when I feel that the Spirit of God is there, then I realize I am sowing the good seed, that it is falling on good ground, and I expect the joyful sheaves that are to be my reward.

Yet, dear believer, we are as much the servants of God when we are doing the one thing as when we are doing the other. We are as much in His service when we are unsuccessful as when we are successful. We are not responsible to God for the souls that are saved, but we are responsible for the Gospel that is preached and for the way in which we preach it. And who can tell whether those of us who have been least successful may not suddenly exchange our heavy toil for the most delightful service? We do not know *"what a day may bring forth."*

And how do you know, my fellow believer, what may yet happen? Perhaps you said this very morning, "It is a dark age for the church!" Well, so it is. Perhaps you said, "I believe it is quite a crisis." So it is. Every year, in fact, seems to be a crisis. "Yes," you say, "but there are exceptional dangers now." No doubt there are, and I think that your oldest relative could recollect that there were exceptional dangers when he or she was a child. There always have been and always will be exceptional dangers.

Presently, we are in danger from a revival of ritualism. Yet, which one of us can tell *"what a day may bring forth"*? Are we certain that God will not yet turn back the tide of error? Are we sure that He does not have a man somewhere, or even fifty men, who will be the instrument of this? Has it not often occurred that the very men who were the most outspoken advocates of a certain system have afterward been the very greatest enemies of that system? The Christian church could never have expected to get an apostle from among the Pharisees; least of all could they have supposed that Saul of Tarsus, the bloodthirsty persecutor, would be the great apostle to the Gentiles, not one bit behind the very greatest of the Twelve. You and I do not know what God has in store.

Somewhere, at this very moment, there may be a man who is reading the Word, and, as he reads it, he may be in the same position as the monk Martin Luther. He may get such light through the reading that, though he once helped build up heresy, he will be the instrument in God's hand to destroy it. I am getting more and more hopeful about these matters. I entertain the most optimistic expectation that the God who has defeated His enemies in years gone by will do it now once again. Instead of sitting down in anything like heaviness of spirit or oppression of heart, I speak hopefully. I want you, my fellow believer, to feel hopeful, for we do not know *"what a day may bring forth."* In one moment, the whole current of the public mind may be turned.

There may come a great tide of conversions that will be the strength and the joy of the Christian church. All of a sudden, slumbering churches may awake, gracious revivals may come to our land, and the holy fire may once again descend from heaven. The Christian church may wake up to find that the God who answered by fire is still in her midst. The mourning Christian may put off his ashes and sackcloth and put on his beautiful array. A shout of joy may go up—"Hallelujah! Hallelujah!"—where you and I expected to hear nothing but "Crucify Him! Crucify Him!"

Let us, then, if we are working for the Master, instead of growing tired with service, hear Him say, *"Be* [not] *weary in well doing: for in due season* [you] *shall reap, if* [you] *faint not"* (Gal. 6:9). Let us, beloved believers, be *"stedfast, unmoveable, always abounding in the work of the Lord, forasmuch as ye know that your labour is not in vain in the Lord"* (1 Cor. 15:58). You do not know how soon you will see this success, for you do not know *"what a day may bring forth."* I hope that all who read this—every church member, every missionary, every minister,

58

every Sunday school teacher—will try to look this very sweet thought in the face. Expect that God is going to do great things, and He will do them, for He does much according to His people's expectations. *"According to your faith be it unto you"* (Matt. 9:29).

Those Discouraged in Prayer

I would like to write a few paragraphs to those who are disheartened in prayer. Perhaps you have engaged in special supplication for something, but up until now you have received no answer, and you are ready to give up. Let me encourage you to persevere by repeating to you the words of Solomon: *"Thou knowest not what a day may bring forth."*

There is a story told by my Methodist friends about a woman who had prayed for a long time for her husband's salvation. She resolved that she would pray for him a certain number of times every day for, I think, ten years. She decided that after that she would pray no longer, supposing that if her prayers were not heard by that time, it would be an indication that God did not intend to grant the blessing. I do not think she was right in setting any limit on God at all, or that she had any right to act this way. However, on this occasion, God overlooked His servant's fault, and, so the story goes—and I do not doubt its truth—on the day she was to cease from prayer, her husband suddenly became thoughtful and asked her the question that she had so longed to hear: *"What must I do to be saved?"* (Acts 16:30).

I am sure that you who have monitored your success in prayer could tell stories just as startling as that one—things that your neighbor would not believe if you were to tell him, but that you treasure, nonetheless, because they are true. You know, dear friend, that you have obtained answers to prayer, very extraordinary ones, and have obtained them very promptly and in a timely manner. You have had your prayers met just as an honest businessman pays his bills—on time. On the expected day, God has met with you and given you what you needed. He has given you what you sought, just at the very time you needed it.

I imagine that many of my readers are being tried. That dear child of yours, instead of rewarding your prayers, seems to be going from bad to worse. Perhaps, dear believer, it is your son—and I know there are many such cases. The Devil has told you that it is no use to pray for him, for God will never hear you. Or else, it is your brother, and your prayers for him have been incessant; indeed, his lost state has been a constant burden on your mind. Now, in such cases, I charge you, I earnestly entreat you, never to listen to the malicious lie of Satan that you may as well stop praying because you will not be heard. For, at the very least—and I am now putting it on the very lowest ground possible—*thou knowest not what a day may bring forth.*" The hard heart may yet soften, and the rebellious heart may yet be subdued.

You would be surprised to go home and find your son converted, would you not? Well, such things have occurred. You would be surprised if your wife came in some Sunday evening and said, "I have been listening to so-and-so, and God has met with me." Yet, why should it not happen? Is anything too hard for the Lord? Is His arm *"shortened, that it cannot save,"* or His *"ear heavy, that it cannot hear"* (Isa. 59:1)? Even if you should die without seeing your children converted, you do not know even then *"what a day may bring forth."* They may be converted after you are dead. Perhaps it would enlarge your joy in heaven to see them brought to follow in the footsteps of their godly father after years of wandering. Children might despise a godly father while he is living but come to imitate him after he is gone.

Persevere in prayer, Christian. *"Men ought always to pray, and not to faint"* (Luke 18:1). Breath spent in prayer is never spent in vain. Still besiege the throne. The city may hold out for a while, but prayer will capture it. Surround the throne of grace with your prayers; it is to be taken. Never end the siege until you get the blessing. The blessing will certainly be yours.

Those Who Are Happy

I will close this chapter with one other thought to those who are cheerful and happy.

I hope there are many readers who are neither afraid and fretting about the future, nor depressed about the present; neither worn-out with toil in the Master's service, nor dispirited in prayer. There are some of us to whom the Lord is so gracious that our cups run over.

Now, I hope that my words will put yet another drop on the top of the full cup. Dear friend, *"thou knowest not what a day may bring forth."* It may perhaps bring forth to you and to me our last day. What a blessed day that would be—our last day! Our dying day! No, let us not call it our dying day, but let us call it the day of our translation, the day of our great change, the day of our being taken up, the day of our being carried away in the fiery chariot to be forever with the Lord! It is not very far from here to heaven.

Recently, one Christian woman in my congregation unexpectedly went from here to heaven in a minute, no, less than that. It is not far to heaven. A sigh will take us there. If we were merely to stop breathing, we would be there.

> One gentle sigh the fetters breaks,
>   We scarce can say "they're gone";
> Before the willing spirit takes
>   Her mansion near the throne.

The journey occupies no time. When we leave the body, we are at once forever with the Lord. There is no tarrying on the road, no quarantine in which we will be delayed for an interval before we are allowed to enter heaven. Christ said to the dying thief, *"To day shalt thou be with me in paradise"* (Luke 23:43). Once we leave the earth, we are found in heaven. When we close our eyes below, we open them in the world above.

You do not know whether this may be your case tomorrow. Oh, what joy! I am doubting and fearing today, but I may see His face tomorrow and never lose sight of it again. From my place of poverty I am going to the mansions of eternal blessedness. From the sickbed, where I have tossed and turned in pain, I will mount to everlasting joy. The streets of gold may be walked upon tomorrow, and the palm branch of victory may be waved tomorrow—walked upon by these weary feet and waved by these weary hands tomorrow.

Yes, tomorrow the chants of angels may be in your ears, and the swell of celestial music may make glad your soul. Tomorrow you may know God as only those in heaven know Him; you may behold the King in His beauty in the land that is very far away. I do like to live in the constant anticipation of being with

Christ, *"which is far better"* (Phil. 1:23). Do not think of death, Christian, as being far away. If we had to wait a hundred years, they would soon pass like a watch in the night. But we will not live that many years longer. We may be with our Lord tomorrow. We may eat dinner here on earth, and breakfast in heaven. We may hear Christ say, *"Come and dine"* (John 21:12), and go from our table here to the great Supper of the Lamb above, to be with Him forever, world without end.

When somebody once said to a Christian minister, "I suppose you are on the wrong side of fifty?" he said, "No, thank God, I am on the right side of fifty, for I am sixty and am therefore nearer heaven." Old age should never be looked upon with dismay by us; it should be our joy. If our hearts were right in this matter, instead of being at all afraid at the thought of parting from this life, we would say,

> Ah me! ah me that I
> In Kedar's tents here stay!
> No place like this on high!
> Thither, Lord! guide my way.
>   O happy place!
>   When shall I be,
>   My God, with Thee,
>   And see Thy face?

We should be looking for the coming of our Lord and waiting for His appearing, feeling that we do not know *"what a day may bring forth."*

Those Who Are Thoughtless about the Future

Unfortunately, there are some reading this book who cannot share in these sweet themes. Let me at

63

least say this: let the careless and thoughtless remember that they do not know *"what a day may bring forth."*

Tomorrow you may not be able to attend that party to which you plan to go. Tomorrow you may have no chance to commit that sweet sin that your evil nature is pondering. Tomorrow may see you on a sickbed. Tomorrow may see you on your deathbed. Tomorrow, worst of all, may see you in hell! Oh, sinner, what a state to live in, to be in daily jeopardy of eternal ruin, to have the wrath of God, who is always angry with you (Ps. 7:11), abiding on you. What a state to live in, to know that tomorrow you may be where you can find no escape, no hope, no comfort. Tomorrow in eternity! Tomorrow banished from His presence! Tomorrow to have that awful sentence vibrating in your soul: *"Depart from me, ye cursed, into everlasting fire, prepared for the devil and his angels"* (Matt. 25:41).

> Come guilty souls, and flee away
> Like doves to Jesu's wounds;
> This is the welcome gospel-day,
> In which free grace abounds.
>
> God loved the church, and gave His Son
> To drink the cup of wrath:
> And Jesus says, He'll cast out none
> That come to Him by faith.

Chapter 4

Christ Frees Us from Infirmities

Behold, there was a woman which had a spirit of infirmity eighteen years, and was bowed together, and could in no wise lift up herself. And when Jesus saw her, he called her to him, and said unto her, Woman, thou art loosed from thine infirmity. And he laid his hands on her: and immediately she was made straight, and glorified God.
—Luke 13:11–13

Our text commences with a *behold*—"*Behold, there was a woman.*" As was often remarked by the Puritan writers, whenever we see the word *behold* in Scripture, we are to regard it as a signal, calling our particular attention to what follows. Where Christ worked wonders, we should have attentive eyes and ears. When Jesus is dispensing blessings, whether to ourselves or to others, we should never be in a state of indifference.

I will use this miracle as a type, as it were, for doubtless the miracles of Christ were intended to be used this way. Our Lord was declared to be "*a prophet mighty in deed and word*" (Luke 24:19). In this He was a prophet like Moses, and, in fact, He is the only one like Moses in these two respects. Many prophets who came after Moses were mighty in word—such as Jeremiah, Ezekiel, and Isaiah—however, they were not mighty in deed. Many, on the other hand, were mighty in deed—like Elijah and Elisha—but they were not mighty in word. Our Lord was mighty in both respects, and He was a prophet in both respects—*"a prophet mighty in deed and word"* (Luke 24:19).

I take it, therefore, that His miraculous deeds are parts of His prophecies. They are the illustrations of His great life sermon. The words that fell from His lips are like the text of a book, but the miracles are like the pictures, from which our child-like minds may often learn more than from the words themselves.

We will use the picture before us now, the picture of the woman with *"a spirit of infirmity."* May the Holy Spirit use it to instruct us.

The Poor Woman's Plight

In the first place, this woman who was bent over because of *"a spirit of infirmity"* typifies to us the case of very many. Oh, that the same miracle might be performed in others as it was in her.

Similar Sufferers

There are people who are depressed in spirit, who cannot look up to heaven and rejoice in the Lord Jesus Christ. There are people who have a hope, a good hope, too, but not a strong one. They have a hope that enables them to hold on long enough to survive, as the sailors did in Paul's shipwreck, when on the boards and broken pieces of the ship they came safely to land. However, they do not have a hope that gives them an abundant entrance into the kingdom of our Lord and Savior Jesus Christ. They are saved—like this woman who was a true daughter of Israel, notwithstanding all her infirmities. She was truly of the promised seed, even though she could not lift herself up. In the same way, these are genuine Christians, truly saved, yet constantly subject to infirmity.

Some find themselves depressed because of their fear of the unpardonable sin. They believe in Christ and rest on the precious blood, yet they are afraid sometimes that they have committed the unpardonable sin. Though their better and more reasonable selves will do battle against this delusion, still they hug it to their hearts.

They do not understand that, because blasphemy against the Holy Spirit is *"a sin unto death"* (1 John 5:16), when a man has committed it, his spirit dies. Repentance, the desire to be saved, and all good emotions cease to exist when that dreadful spiritual death occurs. Thus, a person who commits the unpardonable sin does not even have a desire to be saved. Using such facts, these depressed people can reason with themselves in their better moments and see that their fear is a delusion. But then they fall back again into that dreadful dejection. They do not see signs of grace, but they think they see signs of damnation.

I have met with many people like this. I meet with such people every week who are afraid that they are hypocrites. When I encounter people troubled with this fear, I cannot help smiling at them, for if they really were hypocrites, they would not be afraid of being one. Their fear of presumption argues very strongly that they are not living in it.

Sometimes this infirmity takes another shape. If you steer certain believers away from the other errors, they say they are afraid that they are self-deluded. This is a very proper fear when it leads to self-examination and comes to an end, but it becomes a very improper fear when it perpetually destroys our joy, prevents our saying, *"Abba, Father"* (Rom. 8:15) with an unfaltering tongue, and keeps us at a distance from the precious Savior. Jesus wants us to come very near to Him and be most familiar with His brotherly heart.

Even if this difficulty should be met and overcome, still there are tens of thousands who are very much in doubt about their salvation. They continually ask, What if I am not one of the elect? This, of course, results from ignorance, for if they would read the Word, they would soon discover that all those who believe in Christ may be certain of their election, faith being the public mark of God's privately chosen people. If you make your calling sure, you have made your election sure. If you know that you are now a lover of God, resting upon the great atonement that Jesus has made for sin, then you may know that this is a work of grace in your soul. God has never done a work of grace where He has not already made an election of grace. That fear, therefore, may be easily driven away, yet tens of thousands are in bondage to it.

Others are afflicted with the daily fear that they will not persevere. They say, "After all my professions and prayers, I will yet be a castaway!" The apostle Paul was not afflicted with this fear. He strove, lest this fear should ever come near him. He lived with holy diligence so that he could always live in a state of blessed assurance, lest after having preached to others he himself should be a castaway (1 Cor. 9:27). He could say, *"I know that my redeemer liveth"* (Job 19:25), even as Job could, and he could also say, *"I know whom I have believed, and am persuaded that he is able to keep that which I have committed unto him against that day"* (2 Tim. 1:12).

Still, tens of thousands are perpetually subject to that form of bondage. They cannot seem to reach the full assurance of faith. They barely have even a glimmer of assurance. They do trust; they trust as the publican did—*"standing afar off"* (Luke 18:13)—but they have never yet come with John to lean their heads upon the bosom of the Savior. They are His disciples and His servants, but they can scarcely understand how He can call them His friends and permit close communion with Himself.

The Specifics of Her Case

Now, beloved, this woman who was bent over was very much like these people for the following reason: her infirmity marred her beauty. The beauty and dignity of the human form is to walk erect, to look at the sun, and to gaze upon the heavens. This woman could do none of these things. She was, no doubt, very conscious of this, and she shrank from the public gaze. In the same way, unbelief, distrust, and suspicion—these dreadful infirmities to which some are subjected—spoil these people's spiritual beauty. They have the grace of humility; in this they very often excel others. But the other graces—the noble graces of faith and holy confidence and courage—these they cannot display. The beauty of their character is marred.

Moreover, this woman's enjoyment of life was spoiled. It must have been a sad thing for her to go around bent double! She could not gaze on the beauties of nature as others could, and all her motions certainly must have been extremely inconvenient, if not painful. Such is the case with the doubting, distrustful soul who is struggling with infirmity. He can do little. Prayer is a painful groaning out of his soul. When he sings, it is usually in a deep bass. His harp hangs upon the willows. He feels that he is in Babylon and cannot sing the song of Zion (Ps. 137:2–4).

> Ah! woe is me,
> That I a dweller am
> In Kedar's tents so long!

He might chant such a song as this, but his voice cannot reach the bolder and more jubilant notes of Christian psalms.

Furthermore, this woman must have been very unfit for active service. She could perform very few household duties, and even those caused her pain. As to public acts of mercy, she could take only a small part in them, being subject to this constant infirmity. It is the same way with you who are fearful, you who have troubled spirits. You cannot lead the army in the day of battle. You can scarcely tell others of the Savior's preciousness. You cannot expect to be great reapers in the Master's harvest. You have to stay by the supplies, and there is a special law that David made concerning those who remained there (1 Sam. 30:21–25). So you do get a blessing, but you miss the higher blessing of noble activity and Christian service.

I could continue to show the similarities between this woman and those who are depressed, but I think you can paint the picture for yourself. When you read about the woman coming into the synagogue, your pity is at once aroused. But if you love the souls of men, if God has caused you to be as tender as a nursing mother toward others, you will have even more pity for many Christians who are currently bent over with infirmity.

Now, it appears from our Savior's words that this woman's infirmity was coupled with satanic influence. *"Whom Satan hath bound,"* He said, *"lo, these eighteen years"* (Luke 13:16). We do not know how much Satan has to do with our infirmities. I do know that we often lay a great deal on his back that he does not deserve, and that we do a thousand evil things ourselves and then ascribe them to him. Still, there are gracious souls who do walk in the paths of holiness, who do hate sin, but, for all that, cannot enjoy peace sometimes. We cannot blame them; we must believe that the satanic spirit is at work, marring their joy and spoiling their comfort. Dr. Watts said,

> He worries whom he can't devour,
> With a malicious joy.

Doubtless, that is true. He knows he cannot destroy you because you are in Christ. Therefore, if the dog cannot bite, he will at least bark. You will often be attacked by the evil ones, and all the more so because these evil ones know that in a little while you will be out of gunshot of all the powers of hell, and beyond the hearing of all the roars of the fiends of the pit. Satan has much to do with our problems.

It is also very clear from the passage that the woman's weakness was beyond all human ability to cure. She *"could in no wise lift up herself,"* which implies, I think, that she had tried all the ways within her reach and knowledge. She *"could in no wise."* Neither by those operations that had sometimes been found effective in such diseases, nor by

71

those medicines that were highly recommended in that day, could she receive the slightest relief. She had done her best, and perhaps physicians had tried to help her but had made her worse. Yet, notwithstanding all, she could by no means lift herself up.

Truly, there are many in this spiritual condition. Have you ever been baffled as a Christian pastor, utterly baffled, in dealing with some cases of spiritual distress? Have you ever gone to pray, feeling the blessedness of prayer all the more because you have proved the futility of your own efforts to comfort a sin-distressed, Satan-tossed soul?

Often that has been my case. Even though there was a promise to fit the case, the poor soul could not lay hold of it. Even though the encouraging word had been effective enough at other times, it seemed to be a dead letter to this poor imprisoned spirit. Even though there was the experience of somebody else just like the case at hand, even though I tried to tell it with sympathy, it seemed to do no good. I tried to work myself, as it were, into the position of the person with whom I was dealing, but still I seemed to be speaking to the wind. I seemed to be comforting one who was so accustomed to sorrow that he felt that for him to cast off his heavy burdens would be a sin, and to cease to mourn would be presumption. Many times such a case has come before me, and I have thought of this woman who was bent over. I could only pray that the Master would put His hand upon the person, for my hand and my voice were utterly powerless.

Poor soul, she had been in this situation a long time. Eighteen years! Well, that is not very long if you are in health and strength and prosperity. How the years trip along as if they had wings on their heels! They are scarcely here before they are gone!

72

But eighteen years of infirmity, pain, and constantly increasing weakness! Eighteen years she dragged her chain until the iron entered into her soul. Eighteen years!

Yes, some such people, though *"prisoners of hope"* (Zech. 9:12), are kept in bondage as long as that. Their disease is like an intermittent fever that comes on sometimes and then is relieved. They have times when they are at their worst—the ebb tide—and then they have their floods again. Now and then they have a glimpse of summer, and then the cold winter swiftly comes upon them. Sometimes they half think they have escaped, and they leap like the emancipated slave when his fetters are broken, but they have to go back again very soon to the shackles and the manacles, having no permanent relief, remaining as prisoners year after year. I am probably describing a case that is known to you. Perhaps I am describing you yourself.

Yet, in spite of all this, the woman was a daughter of Abraham. The Lord Jesus knew her ancestry and assured the ruler of the synagogue of it. She was one of the true seed of Israel, notwithstanding all her failings. *"Ought not this woman, being a daughter of Abraham…[to] be loosed from this bond on the sabbath day?"* (Luke 13:16), demanded the Master.

Yes, and you, poor anxious spirit, if you have a simple faith in Christ, even if it is as small as a mustard seed, you are safe. Troubled and tossed one, though your ship seems ready to be swallowed up by the waves, if you have taken Jesus into the vessel, you will come safely to land. Poor heart, you may be brought very low, but you will never be brought low enough to perish, for underneath you are the everlasting arms (Deut. 33:27). Like Jonah, you may go to the bottoms of the mountains, you may think that

73

the earth with her bars is around you forever (Jonah 2:6), but you will yet be brought up, and you will sing Jonah's song: *"Salvation is of the LORD"* (Jonah 2:9).

God does not cast off His people because of their dark moods and feelings. He does not love them because of their high joys, nor will He reject them because of their deep depressions. Every Christian is dear to God, even the limping, the fearful, and the doubting.

What We Learn from Her Example

I must go on to my next topic, namely, that the example of this woman is instructive to everyone in her situation.

She Did Her Best

Observe, she did not yield to her infirmity tamely, and without effort. The expression, *"could in no wise lift up herself,"* shows, as I have said before, that she had tried her best.

I believe that some people in this condition could stand upright if they wanted to. I am quite certain that in some cases people grow accustomed to surrendering to depression, until at last they become powerless against it. Ironically, if some stimulant is given to them in the form of a sick husband or a dying child, they grow quite cheerful. Under some real trouble, they become patient, but when this real trouble is taken away, they begin manufacturing troubles of their own. They are never happy, I must say, except when they are miserable, and never cheerful except when they have something to cast them down. If they have a real trouble, they are able to get strength, but at other times they are morbidly troubled in spirit.

Now, let us imitate this woman and shake off our doubts and our unbelief as much as possible. Let us strike up the following hymn:

Begone, unbelief, my Savior is near,
 And for my relief will surely appear!
By prayer let me wrestle, and He will perform;
 With Christ in the vessel I smile at the storm.

Let us say with David, *"Why art thou cast down, O my soul? and why art thou disquieted in me? hope thou in God: for I shall yet praise him"* (Ps. 42:5). Do not yield so soon to the darts of unbelief. Hold up the shield of faith, and say to your soul, "As the Lord lives, who is the rock of my salvation, my castle and my high tower, my weapon of defense and my glory, I will not yield to unbelief. *'Though he slay me, yet will I trust in him'* (Job 13:15). Though all things go against me, I will sustain myself by trusting the mighty God of Jacob, and I will not fear!"

She Went to Church

Note, next, that although she was bent double and therefore had an excellent excuse for staying at home, she was found at the synagogue. I believe she was always found there, for the length of the time of her illness was well-known—not merely known to Christ because of His divinity, but also known as a matter of common talk and common knowledge in the synagogue. Probably, during the entire eighteen years of her infirmity, she had been in attendance there. "Ah," she must have thought, "even though I miss the blessing of health, I will not be absent from

75

the place where God's people meet together for worship. I have had sweet joys from the singing of the psalms and from listening to the devotions, and I will not stay away when such grace is being dispensed."

Oh, mourner, never let Satan prevail upon you to forsake *"the assembling of* [y]*ourselves together, as the manner of some is"* (Heb. 10:25). If you cannot find comfort, still go to the sanctuary. It is the likeliest place for you to get it. One of the precious traits of character in mourners is that they do go to the assemblies of God's people. I knew one aged woman who had been in depression year after year, and after trying a long time to comfort her, but in vain, I said to her, "Well, why do you go to the house of prayer? Why don't you stay at home?"

"Why, that is my only comfort!" she replied.

"I thought you told me you were a hypocrite," I answered, "and that you had no right to any of the good promises."

"Ah, but I could not stay away from the place where my best friends and my family dwell," she replied.

"And do you read your Bible? I suppose you have burned that?"

"Burned my Bible!" she said in horror. "I'd sooner be burned myself!"

"But do you read it? You say there is nothing there for you. You say that if you were to lay hold of the promises, it would be presumption. You are afraid to grasp any single one of the good things of the covenant!"

"Ah, but I could not do without reading my Bible. That is my daily bread, my constant food," she responded.

"But do you pray?"

"Pray? Oh yes! I will die praying."

"But you told me that you had no faith at all, that you are not one of God's people, that you are a deceiver, among other things."

"Yes, I am afraid sometimes that I am. I am afraid now that I am, but as long as I live I'll pray."

All the marks of a child of God were in her private character and could be seen in her walk and conversation, yet she was always bowed down with depression and could by no means lift herself up.

I remember a fellow minister who was the instrument, in God's hands, of comforting a woman when she lay dying. This woman had always been in the plight of depression. He said to her, "Well, Sarah, you tell me you do not love Christ at all. Are you sure that you do not?"

"Yes, sir. I am sure I do not."

He went to the table and wrote on a piece of paper, "I do not love the Lord Jesus Christ." "Now, Sarah," he said, "just put your name at the bottom of that."

"What is it, sir? I do not know what it is." When she read it, she said, "No, I'd rather be torn in pieces than put my name to such a thing as that!"

"Well," he said, "if it is true, you may write it as well as say it." This was the means of persuading her that there really was love for Christ in her soul after all. But in many cases you cannot comfort these poor souls at all. They will say that they are not the Lord's people, yet they still cling to the means of grace. I trust they will eventually get deliverance.

She Came at Once

I would like you to notice something else. Though we are not told it in so many words in the narrative,

77

we may be sure that it is true. When the Lord Jesus called her, she came at once. She was called, and there was no hesitation in her answer. Such speed as she could make in her poor, pitiable plight, she made. She did not say, as another said, *"Lord, if thou wilt, thou canst"* (Matt. 8:2). She did not doubt His will. Nor did she imitate another and say, *"If thou canst do any thing, have compassion"* (Mark 9:22). She did not doubt His power. She said nothing, but we know what she felt. There is not a trace of unbelief. There is every sign of obedience here.

Now, soul, when Christ calls you by His power, hurry and run to Him. When, under the preaching of the Word, you feel as though the iceberg were beginning to melt, do not get away from the sunlight and go back to the old winter gloom. "Make hay while the sun shines," the old proverb says. Take care that you do so. When God gives you a little light, prize it. Thank Him for it, and ask for more. If you have gotten starlight, ask for moonlight. When you have gotten moonlight, do not sit down and weep because it is only moonlight, but ask Him for more. Then He will give you sunlight. When you have gotten that, be grateful, and He will give you even more. He will make your day to be like the light of seven days (Isa. 30:26), and the days of your mourning will be ended. Think much of little mercies, since you deserve none. Do not throw away these pearls because they are not the greatest that were ever found. Keep them, thank God for them, and then soon He will send you the best treasures from the jewel box of His grace.

She Glorified God

As soon as this woman was healed, she was in another respect an example to us; namely, she glorified

78

God. Her face glorified God. With what luster was it lit up! Her movements glorified God. How erect she stood! And I am sure her tongue glorified God. Restored as she was all of a sudden, she could not help but tell the joy she felt within. The bells of her heart were ringing merry peals; she had to give glory to God who had worked the cure.

You may profess to have been cured, but have you given glory to God? Why, you may profess to be a Christian yet have never come forward to acknowledge it! You have been afraid to unite yourself with the Christian church. Your Master tells you to confess Him. The mode of confession that He prescribes is that you be baptized in His name. Though He has saved you, you stand back and are disobedient. Be careful! *"That servant, which knew his lord's will, and prepared not himself, neither did according to his will, shall be beaten with many stripes"* (Luke 12:47).

This week I was by the bedside of a dying man, an heir of heaven, washed in Christ's precious blood, and rejoicing in it, too. Yet he could not help saying, "Years ago I should have taken my stand with God's people. You have often given me many hard blows through your preaching, but never too hard. Tell the people, when you speak to them again, never to postpone a duty once they know that they should do it. That word is true, *'That servant, which knew his lord's will, and prepared not himself, neither did according to his will, shall be beaten with many stripes.'* I am not condemned, and I am not cast away. Indeed, I am in Christ. I am resting on the precious blood, and I am saved. But, though saved, I am being chastened."

If you are God's child, any duty neglected will bring upon your soul some chastisement. If you are not God's child, you may do very much as you like, and your punishment will perhaps not come upon you until the next world. But if you are the King's favorite, you must walk very humbly and very attentively, or else, as surely as you are dear to the heart of God, you will feel the rod upon you to chasten you and to bring you back into the path of obedience.

This woman glorified God. Fellow believer, can we not do something more to glorify God than we have already done? If we have done what seemed to be our duty on certain occasions, may there not be yet more? There is very much land yet to be possessed for King Jesus. Our cities are given over to sin, and we are doing so little! Ah, some of you do what you can. But we who do what we can might do more if we had more strength with which to do it, and more strength is to be had for the asking. Oh, that we could enlarge our desires for the glory of King Jesus! Oh, to set Him upon a glorious high throne, to crown Him with many crowns, to prostrate ourselves at His feet, and to bring others to be prostrate at His feet, too. Oh, that He might be King of Kings and Lord of Lords, reigning in our souls forever and ever. Imitate this woman. If you have been weighed down and yet restored to comfort, see that, like her, you instantly begin to glorify God.

Lessons for Those in a Similar Condition

And this brings me to the last topic. The woman's cure is very instructive to people in a similar situation.

She went to the synagogue, but she did not get her cure just by going there. Means and ordinances are nothing in themselves. They are to be used, but they are only empty bottles without water, unless there is something more. This woman met with Christ in the synagogue, and then her healing came. May we, too, meet with Jesus. That great encounter is possible in church or anywhere, for

Where'er we seek Him He is found,
And every place is hallowed ground.

The important thing is to meet with Him. If we meet with Him, we meet with all that we need.

Now, notice the woman's cure. In the first place, it was a complete cure. No part of the infirmity remained. She was not left a little crooked. No, she was made straight. When Jesus heals, He does not heal halfway. It may be said of each of His works of grace, *"It is finished"* (John 19:30). Salvation is a finished work throughout.

In the next place, the woman's cure was a perpetual and permanent one. She did not return to be healed again of a terrible relapse of her former condition. Once she was made to walk upright, she remained so. Likewise, when Jesus sheds abroad life, love, and joy in the soul, they are ours for a perpetual inheritance; we may hold them until we die, and we will not lose them then.

Notice, too, that the woman was healed immediately. That is a point that Luke took care to mention. The cure did not take days, weeks, months, or years, as physicians' cures do, but she was cured immediately. Here is encouragement for you who have been depressed for years. There is still a possibility that you may be perfectly restored. The dust may yet be taken from your eyes; your face may yet be anointed with fresh oil; you may yet glow and glisten in the light of Jesus' countenance, while you reflect the light that shines upon you from Him. It may happen today, at this moment! Gates may be taken off their hinges, for if the mighty Jesus whom we serve wills it, He can tear off Gaza's gates—posts, bars, and all (Judg. 16:3)—to set His captives free.

Even if you are bound by all the shackles that self can forge, at one word from Christ, one emancipating word, you will be entirely free. As John Bunyan showed us in *The Pilgrim's Progress*, Doubting Castle may be very strong, but He who comes to fight with Giant Despair is stronger still. He who has kept you beneath his power is mighty, but the Almighty will conquer in every place where He comes forth for the deliverance of His people. Take down your harps from the willows (Ps. 137:1–4)! Be encouraged. Jesus Christ releases the prisoners. He is the Lord, the Liberator. He comes to set the captives free and to glorify Himself in them.

The woman's restoration was brought about by Jesus Christ—by His laying His hands upon her. Many of His cures were worked in this way, by bringing His own personality into contact with human infirmity. *"He laid his hands on her."* Oh, friend, Christ came in human flesh, and that contact with humanity is the source of all salvation. If you believe in Christ, He comes into contact with you. Oh, that your soul might get a touch from Him even now! He is a man like yourself, though He is very God of very God.

Christ suffered unutterable pains. The whole weight of our sin was laid upon Him until He was bruised beneath the wheels of the vehicle of vengeance. Beneath the upper and lower millstone of divine vengeance, the Savior was ground like fine flour. God knows, and God alone knows, what agonies He bore.

All this was substitutionary for sinners. Do not let your sins, then, depress you. If you had no sin, you would not need a Savior. Come with your sin, and trust in Him. Do not let your weakness distress you. If you had no weakness, you would not need a mighty Savior. Come and take hold of His strength, for all His strength is meant for the weak, the hopeless, and the helpless. Sitting on the trash heap of your sin, trust in Jesus, and you will be lifted up to dwell among the princes of royal blood.

God must indeed have power to save, since He became man to bleed and die. Nothing can be impossible to Him who built the world, who bears the pillars of it upon His shoulders, and who yet gives His hands to the nails and His side to the spear. Nothing can be impossible to Emmanuel, God with us, when He aches, groans, and submits to the bloody sweat, and then empties out His heart's blood so that He might redeem men from their iniquities.

> Oh! come all ye in whom are fixed
> The deadly stains of sin!

Draw near to the Crucified One. Let your soul contemplate Christ. Let your faith look to Him. Let your love embrace Him. Cast away all other confidences as mere vanities that will delude you. Away with them! Trust in nothing but the Lord Jesus Christ—His person, His work, His life, His death, His resurrection, His ascension, His glorious pleading before the throne for sinners such as we are.

Ah, when it comes to dying, you who are strong and you who are depressed will be so much alike in this matter, that you will have to come to the place where Wesley was when he said,

Jesus, lover of my soul,
Let me to Thy bosom fly.

Other refuge have I none;
Hangs my helpless soul on Thee.

You will come to where Toplady stood when he sang,

Nothing in my hands I bring,
   Simply to Thy Cross I cling;
Naked, look to Thee for dress,
   Helpless come to Thee for grace:
Black, I to the fountain fly,
   Wash me, Savior, or I die.

Look to the wounds of Christ; they will heal your wounds. Look to the death of Christ; it will be the death of your doubts. Look to the life of Christ; it will be the life of your hopes. Look to the glory of Christ; it will be the glory of your spirit here and the glory of your spirit forever and ever!

May God add His blessing to these words and bring many in bondage out of prison. This will be to His eternal praise.

Chapter 5

Mercy for the Least of the Flock

In that day, saith the LORD, will I assemble her that halteth, and I will gather her that is driven out, and her that I have afflicted.
—Micah 4:6

I believe that the words of Micah 4:6 were spoken, in the first place, of the Jewish people, who have been greatly afflicted on account of their sin. They are driven here and there among the lands and are made to suffer greatly. However, in the last times, when Christ will appear in His glory in the days of golden peace, Israel will partake of the universal joy. Poor, limping, faltering Israel, afflicted by life's storms, will yet be gathered and will rejoice in her God.

However, I am sure that the text also applies to the church of God, and we will not interpret it wrongly if in it we find promises to individual Christians as well. Therefore, we will regard the text in those two lights, as spoken to the church and as spoken to individual souls.

God's Care for the Church

God says concerning the church, *"In that day...*
will I assemble her that halteth, and I will gather her
that is driven out, and her that I have afflicted."

The Weak Church

The church of God is not always vigorous and
prosperous. Sometimes she can run without weari-
ness and walk without fainting, but at other times
she begins to limp and to hobble. She becomes deficient in her faith or lukewarm in her love. Doctrinal
errors spring up, and many things both weaken and
trouble her. When these things occur, the church
becomes like a lame person. Indeed, beloved, when I
compare the church of God at the present moment
with the first apostolic church, she may well be
called, *"her that halteth."*

Oh, how she leaped in the first Pentecostal
times! What wondrous strength she had throughout
all Judea and all the neighboring lands! The voice of
the church in those days was like the voice of a lion,
and the nations heard and trembled. The farthest
islands of the sea understood the power of the Gospel, and before long the cross of Christ was set up on
every shore. Thus was the church in her early days.
She had the love of a bride, and her strength was
like that of a young wild ox (Ps. 29:6).

How the church halts now! How deficient in
vigor, how weak in her actions! When Christians went
bravely to prison and to the stake to bear witness to
the Lord Jesus, when the truth was held with firm-
ness and proclaimed with earnestness, and when the
truth was lived out by those who professed it—then

the church was mighty. Then the church certainly could not be compared to *"her that halteth,"* as I fear she is now in these days of laxity of doctrine and laxity of life, when error is tolerated in the church and loose living is tolerated in the world.

The church of today is weak in comparison with those early days of Methodism. At that time, George Whitefield was like an angel flying in the midst of heaven, preaching in England and America the unsearchable riches of Christ to tens of thousands. John Wesley and others were working with undiminished fervor to reach the poorest of the poor and the lowest of the low. Those were good days, even with all their faults. Life and fire abounded. The God of Israel was glorified, and tens of thousands were converted. The church seemed as though it had risen from the dead and had cast off its grave clothes and was rejoicing in newness of life.

We are not without hopeful signs today. Everything does not depress us; much encourages us. At the same time, the church limps. She does not stand firm and fast. Oh, that God would be pleased to visit her.

The Suffering Church

Moreover, as I look at the text, I perceive that not only is the church weak at times, but, at the same time, or at some other time, the church is also persecuted and made to suffer. The text speaks of *"her that is driven out."* It has often happened that the church has been driven right out from among men. It has been said of her, *"Away with* [her] *from the earth: for it is not fit that* [s]*he should live"* (Acts 22:22). But how wondrously God has shown His mercy to His people when they have been driven out. The days of exile have been bright days. The sun

87

never shone more beautifully on the church's face than when she worshiped in the catacombs of Rome, when her disciples wandered around in sheepskins and goatskins, destitute, tormented, afflicted.

In England, believers once had to meet in secret. They were perpetually pestered by informers who would bring them before the magistrates for joining in prayer and song. When they got their liberty, they often said that they wished they again lived in the day when they had gathered together in one house and scarcely dared to sing loudly. They had brave times in those days, when every man held his soul in his hand when he worshiped his God, not knowing whether the hand of the hangman or the headsman would soon seize him.

The Lord was pleased to bless His people when the church was driven out. If the snowy peaks of Piedmont, if the lowlands of Holland, if the prisons of Spain could speak, they would tell of infinite mercy experienced by the saints under terrible oppression, of hearts that were leaping in heaven while the bodies were bruised or burning on earth. God has been gracious to His people when they have been driven out.

The Church Afflicted by God

Sometimes trouble comes to God's people in another way. The church is afflicted by God Himself. It seems as if God has put away His church for a time and has driven her from His presence. That has happened often in all churches. Perhaps you are a member of such a church now, or have been. Discord has come in, and the spirit of peace has gone out. Coldness has come into the pulpit, and a chill has come over the pews. The prayer meetings are neglected, and the seeking of souls almost has been given up. The candlestick is there, but the candle seems to be gone, or not to be lighted. Means of grace have become lifeless. You almost dread Sundays, which once were your comfort.

It is wretched for Christian people when the church comes to this. Yet, in dozens of cities and towns, this is the case. The people in the church, the sheep, look to their pastor, the shepherd, but he has no food. The shepherd does not know where to get the food, because he has not been taught by God. It is a melancholy thing wherever this is the case. But I would encourage the saints to cry mightily for the return of God's Spirit, for the restoration of unity and peace, earnestness and prayerfulness. Pray once again for the solitary places of the wilderness to be made glad and for the desolate places to blossom like the rose (Isa. 35:1).

My friend, may God never treat the church as she deserves to be treated, for when I look around and see her sins, they rise up to heaven like a mighty cry. We have been told in so many words, by an eminent preacher, that all creeds have something good in them, even the creed of the heathen, and that out of all of them the grand creed is to be made, which is yet to be the religion of mankind. God save us from those who talk this way and yet profess to be sent by God! They who know in their own souls what God's truth is will not be led astray by such delusions. But God may yet visit His church and chasten her sorely by depriving her of His Spirit for a while. If He has done so, or is about to do so, let us still pray that He may gather her who is driven out and afflicted.

Prayer for the Church

I am eager to share the blessing that will come, in answer to prayer, upon churches that are weak or sorely persecuted. There are scattering times, no doubt, but we should always pray that we may live in gathering times. Pray that we may be gathered together in unity, in essential oneness, around the Cross, in united action for our glorious Master. Pray that sinners who are far away may be gathered in, too, and that backsliders who have wandered may be restored. Pray for gathering times, believer, and may the day come when the Lord will *"assemble her that halteth"* and will *"gather her that is driven out."*

Notice that the text speaks of *"that day."* We may expect that God will have His own time of blessing. *"In that day, saith the LORD, will I assemble her that halteth."* I believe that will be a day in which we will seek after the Lord—a day in which we will be prayerful, in which we will become anxious, in which an agony will lay hold of the souls of believers until the Lord returns unto His people. I believe it will be a day when Christ will be revealed in the testimony of the church and when the Gospel will be fully preached. *"In that day,"* the Lord will *"assemble her that halteth."*

May that day quickly come! But if we do not see the blessing tomorrow, let us remember that tomorrow may not be God's day. Let us persevere in prayer until God's day does come. There are better days in store for the church, and before the pages of human history close, there will be times of triumph for her in which she will be glorious and God will be glorified in her.

God's Care for Individual Believers

I will, however, stop writing about the church and start writing about individual believers, because I wish to speak to mourners—to melancholy ones. I trust I have a message of mercy to some who

90

are despondent. Therefore, we will look at the text, secondly, as referring to individual souls. *"In that day, saith the LORD, will I assemble her that halteth."*

I have been thinking about why the word *her* is used here. Why is the word *him* not used? Surely the blessing is meant for masculine mourners, as well as for feminine ones. I suppose the feminine form is used here because the woman is often the weaker of the two. Therefore, the weaker sex is chosen here to be figurative of the weaker believer. Moreover, our sisters are also the tenderer of the two sexes. They are more sensitive; they often suffer far more acutely than men do. They have tender spirits; they are not rough and of a coarse mold as men often are. So the Lord looks upon His people in their sensitivity, and He says, "Poor, tender heart, though you have a woman's nature and are full of proneness to sorrow, I will bless you in your weakness and tenderness."

The word *her* is, no doubt, meant to remind us also of the relationship between the Lord Jesus and His people. He is very fond, both in the prophetic books of the Old Testament and in others, of speaking of the church as His bride, His spouse, and of Himself as her husband. Therefore, since the term is full of love, He here addresses each soul in His church, each weak and tried one, as though we were His spouse, and He speaks of us as *"her."*

Now, there are three kinds of Christians described in our text. Let us find each of them.

Weak Christians

First is the soul who halts, that is, the one who is lame. Of course, this describes those Christians who are very weak. Some of God's people are strong—*"strong in the Lord, and in the power of his might"* (Eph. 6:10). It would be a great mercy if all God's people were so. But there are some Christians who have faith of a feeble sort. They do love God, but they sometimes question whether they love Him at all. They have piety in their hearts, but it is not of that vigorous kind that one would desire. It is rather like the spark in the flax, or the music in the bruised reed (Isa. 42:3). They have little faith and are much afraid. They are alive, but scarcely alive. Sometimes their lives seem to tremble in the balance, yet they are hidden with Christ in God (Col. 3:3). Therefore, they are really beyond the reach of harm. But they are the weak ones. And God speaks to such weak ones and says, *"I* [will] *assemble her that halteth."*

They are not only weak, but they are also slow and faltering. A lame person cannot travel quickly. And, oh, how slow some Christians are! What little progress they make in the divine life! They were little children ten years ago, and they are still little children now. Their own children have grown up to be adults, but they themselves do not appear to have made any progress. They are just babes in grace, still needing milk. They are not strong enough to feed on the strong meat of the kingdom of God (Heb. 5:12–14). They are slow to believe all that the prophets and apostles have spoken, slow to rejoice in God, slow to catch a truth and perceive its importance, but slower still to get the nutrients out of it and realize its application to themselves.

But, slow as they are, I trust we may say of them that they are as sure as they are slow. What steps they do take are well taken, and if they come slowly like a snail, yet they are, like the snail in Noah's days, crawling toward the ark and getting in somehow.

With this slowness there is also pain. A lame man walks painfully. Perhaps every time he puts his foot to the ground, a shock of pain goes through his whole system. Some Christians, in their progress in the heavenly life, seem to be afflicted in the same manner. I encounter some Christians who are very sensitive, and every time they do anything wrong they are ashamed and grieved. I wish some other Christians had more of that feeling, for it is an awful fact that many professing Christians seem to tamper much with sin and think nothing of it. To have a sensitive soul that is fearful and timid lest it should in any way grieve the Spirit of God, to have an eye that is watchful and a conscience that is quick and tender, is better than to have presumption and hardness of heart.

However, some have this sensitivity without the other qualities that balance it, and it makes their journey to heaven a safe but a painful one. They do not look enough at the Cross. They do not remember that *"if we walk in the light, as he is in the light, we have fellowship one with another, and the blood of Jesus Christ his Son cleanseth us from all sin"* (1 John 1:7). They do not see that the Lord Jesus Christ is able to deliver us from all sin, so that indwelling sin will not have dominion over us, because we are not under the law but under grace (Rom. 6:14). So their progress is painful. But, beloved, the promise is for them: "*'I* [will] *assemble her that halteth.'* When I call My people together, I will call her, too. When I send an invitation to a feast, I will direct one especially to her. She is weak, she is slow, and she is in pain. But, in spite of all that, *'I* [will] *assemble her.'"*

Our text alludes, perhaps, to a sheep that has somehow been lamed. The shepherd has to get all the flock together, and, therefore, he must bring the lame one in, too. Likewise, the Good Shepherd of the sheep takes care that the lame sheep will be gathered. I find that the original word for *"halteth"* has something of the meaning of one-sidedness. A lame sheep depends heavily on one side. It cannot use one foot, and so it has to throw its weight on the other side.

Many Christians have a one-sidedness in religion, and, unfortunately, that often happens to be the gloomy side. They are very properly suspicious of themselves, but they do not counterbalance that suspicion with confidence in the Lord Jesus Christ. Looking back on their past and seeing their own unfaithfulness, they forget God's faithfulness. Looking at the present, they see their own imperfections and infirmities, and they forget that the Spirit helps our infirmities (Rom. 8:26). If we did not have infirmities, there would be nothing for the Spirit to do but to glorify Himself. When gloomy Christians look ahead to the future, they see the dragons and the dark river of death, but they forget these promises, *"I am with you alway, even unto the end"* (Matt. 28:20), and, *"When thou passest through the waters, I will be with thee"* (Isa. 43:2). What a mercy that the Lord will not forget these one-sided limpers. Christ will assemble them when, with the shepherd's crook, He gathers His flock and brings them home.

We may add to the list of limpers those who have gotten tired because of the trials along the way. It is a weary thing to be lame. It often saddens my heart to see the sheep go down the path. They go limping along, poor things, so spent and spiritless. There are many Christians who are like them; they seem to have been in trouble so long that they do not know how to bear up any longer. With the loss of a husband and the loss of a child, with poverty and many struggles and no apparent hope of deliverance, with one sickness and then another in their own body, with one temptation and then another tempta-tion and then a third, they feel very tired along the way. They are like Jacob when he *"halted upon his thigh"* (Gen. 32:31). What a blessing that the Lord says, *"I* [will] *assemble her that halteth"*!

Grasp that promise, you halting one. I daresay that you think you are the least of the flock. You have gotten so tired and lame that, although all the others are close by the Shepherd's hand, you think you are forgotten. You remember that the Amale-kites in the wilderness attacked the children of Is-rael and killed some of the stragglers in the back of the group, and perhaps you are afraid that you will be struck down in the same way. Let me remind you of a promise from God's Word: *"The LORD will go before you; and the God of Israel will be your rere-ward* [rear guard]" (Isa. 52:12). Now, those who lead the way can rejoice that God goes before them, but you can rejoice that God is behind you, for, *"the glory of the LORD shall be thy rereward* [rear guard]" (Isa. 58:8). He will take care of you so that you will not be destroyed.

> Weak as you are, you shall not faint,
>   Or fainting, shall not die;
> Jesus, the strength of every saint,
>   Will aid you from on high.

He will *"assemble her that halteth."* Does this promise suit your situation? If the medicine meets your disease, take it, and may the Lord use it to bless you.

Exiled Christians

God also takes care of the soul who is exiled. *"I will gather her that is driven out."* Perhaps you have

95

been driven out from the world. It was not a very great world, that world of yours, but still it was very dear to you. You loved your father, mother, brothers, and sisters, but you are like a speckled bird among them now. Sovereign grace and saving love have lighted on you, but not on them. At first they ridiculed you when you went to hear the Gospel, but now that you have received it and they perceive that you are in earnest, they persecute you. You are all by yourself. You almost wish you did not live with them, because you are further away from them than if you were really away from them. Nothing you can do pleases them. They find a thousand faults, and they taunt you when you fail, and say, "So this is your religion!" You cry out, *"Woe is me, that I sojourn in Mesech"* (Ps. 120:5).

Do you recall what became of the man whom the Pharisees cast out? Why, the Lord met him and graciously took him in. The Lord loves His people more when the world hates them. *"If ye were of the world, the world would love his own: but because ye are not of the world, but I have chosen you out of the world, therefore the world hateth you"* (John 15:19). When I go to a man's house and his dog barks at me, it does so because I am a stranger. Likewise, when you go into the world and the world howls at you, it is because you are different from them. They recognize in you the grace of God and pay the only homage that evil is ever likely to pay to goodness; namely, they persecute you with all their might.

Perhaps, however, it is worse than that. "I would not mind being driven out from the world," you say. "I could take that cheerfully, but I seem to be driven out from the church of God." There are two ways in which this may come about. Perhaps you have been zealous for the Lord God of Israel in the midst of a cold church, and perhaps you have not always spoken prudently. The consequence is that you have angered and annoyed the church members, and they have thought that you considered yourself to be better than they, though such a thought was far from your mind. It is an unfortunate thing for a man to be born before his time, yet he may be a great man. Some Christians in certain churches seem to live ahead of their fellow believers. It is a good thing. But as surely as Joseph brought the enmity of his own brothers upon himself because he walked with God and God revealed Himself to him, so is it likely that you, if you are ahead of your brothers in Christ, will bring opposition upon yourself, which will be very bitter. Never mind. If the servants repulse you, go and tell their Master. Do not go around and grumble at them. Ask their Master to mend their manners. He knows how to do it.

However, it is possible that you have been driven out only in your own thoughts. Perhaps the members of your church really love you and think highly of you, but you have become so depressed in spirit that you do not feel that you have any right to be in the church. You have made up your mind that you will not be a hypocrite, and, therefore, you have given up all profession of being a Christian. You have a notion that some of your fellow members think evil of you, and you wonder how a person like you could ever come to the church. Oh, the many poor little lambs that come bleating around me with such troubles! When I tell them, "I have never heard anything against you in my life. I have never heard anybody speak of you except with love and respect. I have never observed anything in you but tenderness of conscience and a quiet, holy walk with God," they seem quite surprised.

Beloved, look after your fellow members. Do not let them think you are cold toward them. Some of them will think that no matter what you may do. Perhaps you are considered to be so proud that you will not look at other people; if they only knew the truth, they would see you are very different.

Now, you lambs, do not be grieved when there is nothing to be grieved about. But you who are stronger than they, be careful that you do not give any offense that can be prevented. *"It must needs be that offences come; but woe to that man by whom the offence cometh!"* (Matt. 18:7). Let us be careful not to break the bruised reed, even by accidentally treading upon it. But, dear brother or sister, if that is your condition, let me tell you that you have not been driven out—it is a mistake. But if you think so, go to your Lord. If you will tell Jesus, He will make up for any apparent change that may come over His people.

Ah, but I think I hear someone say, "It is not being driven out from the world that hurts me, or being driven out from the church. I could bear that. But I have been driven out from the presence of the Lord Himself. I seem to have lost His company, and losing that, I have lost all."

> What peaceful hours I once enjoyed,
> How sweet their memory still!
> But they have left an aching void,
> The world can never fill.

Thank God if you feel like that! If the world could fill your heart, it would prove that you are no child of God, but if the world cannot fill it, then Christ will come and fill it. If you will be satisfied with nothing but Him, He will satisfy you. If you are saying, "I will not be comforted until Jesus comforts me," you will get the comfort. He has never left a soul to perish who was looking to Him and longing for Him. Cry to Him again, and this text will be fulfilled: *"I will gather her that is driven out."* May that word come home to you! I do not know where you may be, but the Master does. May He apply the words to your heart.

Troubled Christians

One other person is mentioned in our text: the soul who is troubled, or *"her that I have afflicted."* Yes, in all churches of God, there are some dear, good friends who are afflicted more than others. They are often the best people. Are you surprised at this? Which vine does the gardener trim the most? The one that bears the most and the sweetest fruit. He uses the knife most upon that one because it pays to prune it, while it scarcely pays to prune some of us! You may be enjoying good health now, but when trial comes, when the Lord prunes you, you can say, "I thank God. He means to do something with me after all."

Perhaps this afflicted one is afflicted in body. He has scarcely a day without pain, scarcely a day without the prospect of more suffering. Well, if there is any child the mother is sure to remember, it is the sick one. And if there are any Christians to whom God is especially close, they are His afflicted ones. I have read concerning the unfortunate, *"Thou wilt make all his bed in his sickness"* (Ps. 41:3). I believe this speaks of sick saints. May the Lord make your bed, dear believer, if you are suffering bodily pain!

Some are mentally afflicted. Much of the doubt and fear we hear about comes from some degree of a mental disorder. The mental trouble may be very

99

slight, but it is very common. I suppose that there is not a perfectly sane person among us. When that great wind blew, about the time of the Fall, a slate blew off everybody's house. Some suffer greater effects than others, causing them to take a negative view of all things. This mental infirmity, which they are not to be blamed for, will be with them until they get to heaven. Well, God blesses those who are mentally troubled.

Then, some are spiritually afflicted. Satan is permitted to try them very much. There is only one way to heaven, but I find that part of the road is a harder path to travel on. Some people seem to go to heaven over the harder path. Their souls are perpetually exercised, while God grants to others to choose the smoother parts of the way and go triumphantly on. Let those I have spoken of hear the word of promise, *"I will gather her...that I have afflicted,"* for when God Himself gives the affliction, He will bring His servant through and glorify Himself by doing so.

The Lord said, *"I will gather her,"* as if to say, "I will gather My tried ones into the fellowship of the church. I will bring My scattered sheep near to Me." The Lord Jesus will gather His dear people to Himself and into fellowship with Himself. He says, "I will gather them every day around My mercy seat. I will gather them one day on the other side of the Jordan, on those green hilltops, where the Lamb will forever feed His people and lead them to living fountains of water."

Poor, tried, lame, afflicted, limping soul, the Shepherd has not forgotten you. He will gather all the sheep, and they will *"pass again under the hands of him that telleth them* [counts them]" (Jer. 33:13). There will not be one missing. I cannot understand

100

how some of my fellow believers think that the Lord will lose some of His people; that there are some whom Jesus has bought with His blood who will get lost on the way! It is an unhappy shepherd who finds some of his lambs devoured by the wolf, but our Shepherd will never be in that predicament with His sheep. *"I give unto them eternal life; and they shall never perish, neither shall any man pluck them out of my hand"* (John 10:28). What do you say to that, you halting ones? What do you say to that, you, the least of all? He has given eternal life to you as much as to the strongest of the flock, and you will never perish, nor will anyone pluck you out of His hand. He will gather you with the rest of them.

The Fulfillment of the Promise

When will He fulfill this promise, beloved? He is always fulfilling it, and He will completely fulfill it the day that He is manifested. When He comes to make peace, as described in the fourth chapter of Micah, when men beat their swords into plowshares, then He will gather you.

Even now, when He comes as the great Peace-giver, He gathers her who halts. When the storms of temptation lie still awhile, and He shows Himself in the heart as the God who walked on the Sea of Galilee long ago, then His people are gathered into peace; they rest in that day. I thank God that the most tried and troubled believer has some gleams of sunlight. Sometimes in the winter there comes a day that looks like a summer day, when the gnats come out and think it is spring, and the birds begin to sing as if they thought that surely the winter were over and past. And in the darkest experience there are always some blessed gleams of light, just enough to keep the soul alive. That is the fulfillment of the promise in one sense: *"In that day...will I assemble her that halteth."*

But the day is coming, yes, the day is coming when you and I who have been limping and feeble and weak will be gathered, never to stumble, never to doubt, and never to sin again. I do not know how long it may be. Perhaps you are much older than I, but we cannot tell whether the youngest or the oldest will go the soonest, for *"many that are first shall be last; and the last shall be first"* (Matt. 19:30). But there is a day, written in the eternal decrees of God, in which we will lay aside every tendency to sin, every tendency to doubt, every capacity for tribulation, and every need for chastisement. Then we will mount up and soar away to the bright world of endless day. What a mercy it will be to find ourselves there! Oh, how we will greet Jesus with joy and gladness and will tell of the redeeming grace and dying love that brought home even the limping ones and the weakest and the feeblest.

I think those who are considered strong and who do the most for God are generally those who consider themselves the weakest when they come to the day of death. I read of a man who had been the means of the conversion of many hundreds of souls by personal, private exertion; his name was Harlan Page. On his deathbed, he said, "They talk of me, but I am nothing, nothing, nothing." He mourned his past life; to him it seemed that he had done nothing for his Master, that his life was a blank. He wept to think he had done so little for Christ, while everyone was wondering how he had lived such a blessed and holy life. The only person who is rich toward God is the one who begins to know his emptiness and feels that he is less than nothing.

Beloved, it is because those who serve God best often feel that they are lame, driven away, afflicted, and tossed with doubts and fears, that this promise is given to the lowest and this blessing to the very least. This is so, in order that those who are strong may yet be able to come when weakened by depression, and say, "That promise will suit me; I will get a grip on it. I will come to God with it in my hand, and at the mercy seat I will get it fulfilled for me, even for me." The Lord says, *"I* [will] *assemble her that halteth, and I will gather her that is driven out, and her that I have afflicted."* The Lord grant you, beloved, to be numbered among His jewels in that day.

Oh, what will I say to those who know nothing about the divine life at all, who, perhaps, are saying, "Well, I never limp or doubt. I have a good time"? Yes, and so does the butterfly while the summer lasts, but the winter kills it. Your summer may last a little while, but the chill of death will soon be on you, and then what is there for you but hopeless misery forever and forever? May God give you grace to fly to Jesus now and be saved with an everlasting salvation, through Jesus Christ our Savior.

Chapter 6

Encouragement for Secret Disciples

*Then the band and the captain and officers
of the Jews took Jesus, and bound him, and led
him away....Annas had sent him bound unto
Caiaphas the high priest. And Simon Peter stood
and warmed himself. They said therefore unto
him, Art not thou also one of his disciples? He
denied it, and said, I am not.*
—John 18:12–13, 24–25

S ome of us consider it our highest joy to answer
yes to the question, *"Art not thou also one of
his disciples?"* We will be glad to endure whatever may result from our confession, but we cannot
do otherwise than say, "Christ acknowledged us long
ago, and He is not ashamed to call us brothers and
sisters; therefore, we are not ashamed of Him, but
we call Him Master and Lord."

I had a conversation about two weeks ago with a
dear and venerable friend who is on the verge of the
grave. He said to me, "There is a verse in the
hymnbook that I know you do not like, and that I do
not like, though both of us have sometimes been
obliged to sing it:

> 'Tis a point I long to know;
> Oft it causes anxious thought:
> Do I love the Lord or no?
> Am I His, or am I not?

But now I do not doubt my love for God any more than I doubt my own existence. Let others doubt if they like. I know I love the Lord; I am sure I do. If there is anything in all this world that is beyond question to me, it is that I do love Him with all my heart and soul and strength."

Now, that ought to be the condition of every Christian. There ought to be no question here. When asked, *"Art not thou also one of his disciples?"* we should be able to reply at once, "I am. I consider it my honor and my joy that He permits me to sit at His feet and to be instructed by Him and to go forth into the world bearing His reproach." But at the same time, dear friend, there are some in the world who could not say all that; nonetheless, we have the hopeful belief that they are His disciples. Their conduct is not that of bold confessors; they are rather like Nicodemus who came to Jesus by night. Like Joseph of Arimathaea, they are disciples, but *"secretly for fear"* (John 19:38). We hope, however, that they are true disciples and that before long they will be open disciples.

I want to write a little to those of you who are not open followers of Christ. Perhaps this will be unfortunate for most of my readers, for I will not be addressing many of them. Still, even if there are only a few like this, I must look after the one at the risk of leaving the ninety-nine. So, if you are suspected of being a follower of Jesus, but your faith needs to show better evidence of it and your life needs to be a little more consistent with being His true follower, then the following words are for you.

Why You Are Suspected of Being a Christian

First, then, I would ask, Why are you suspected of being a disciple of Christ? Now, please observe the reasons that Simon Peter was suspected, for the same reasons may apply to you.

Godly Companions

He was suspected of being Christ's disciple because he had been seen with the other disciples. One of the people asked, *"Did not I see thee in the garden with him?"* (John 18:26). Now, perhaps you are always seen in the house of God, not only at services that are common to the general public, but even at the prayer meeting. You are seen at times when the interest is more spiritual and when only spiritual people, it would be supposed, would be attracted and find anything that would appeal to them. In addition, it is not only in the house of God that you are seen with Christ's people, but also outside the church. You do not enjoy frivolous company, and you do not feel at home in the haunts of vanity. Your companions are the godly. You delight in their conversation, and the more spiritual the conversation, the more you enjoy it.

Now, I do not know for sure that you are a follower of Christ, but I have a strong suspicion that you might be. I would like to ask you these questions, if I might: *"Art not thou also one of his disciples?"* *"Did not I see thee in the garden with him?"* Why do you keep such company and love such companionship if you are not one of them? Is the old proverb not true, "Birds of a feather flock together"? How is it that you love the company of Christians if you are not one of them? I dare not say for sure that you are, for I cannot read your heart; but I will venture to ask the question, *"Art not thou also one of his disciples?"*

Uncommon Conversation

Peter was also suspected of being a disciple because of his conversation. He did not want to be recognized; therefore, I do not suppose that he said anything voluntarily that would have betrayed him. I daresay that if he conversed at all as he warmed himself at the fire, he kept clear of all topics and subjects that would reveal who he was or that would lead to the question of whether he was a disciple or not. But somehow or other, whatever he talked about, there was a sort of dialect, a twang in his speech, a something that showed that, at any rate, he was a Galilean, and they began to suspect that he might also be a companion of Jesus of Nazareth. It was his talk that betrayed him.

Now, I do not know, dear friend, whether you are a disciple of Christ, and I will not press you, but please excuse me for making some observations. I imagine your language and accent have a seasoning and a flavor of Christianity. You earnestly put aside from your speech everything unclean, and you delight to speak words that honor Christ. If at any time in conversation there is a word said that seems to reflect poorly upon the Lord, you are grieved about it, and you would not repeat any sentiment or sentence that would dishonor Him. You are cautious and careful, too, to be truthful in what you say. You desire also to speak good of others. Especially during the last few months you have been very careful, and your prayer has been, *"Open thou my lips"* (Ps. 51:15). You have been afraid of speaking those idle words for which God will bring men into judgment (Matt. 12:36).

Now, I do not know for sure that you are His disciple, but I suspect it, for a man is judged by his speech. We generally know what is in the well by what comes up in the bucket; and the metal of a bell can be pretty well judged by the stroke of the clapper. I think we can form some opinion of you when we perceive in your conversation the tone of a Christian, when we hear you speak as one whose heart has been renewed by divine grace. Therefore, I will ask you the question, expecting a good answer, *"Art not thou also one of his disciples?"*

Holy Zeal

Furthermore, I suspect that Peter was recognized as the one who had just acted for his Lord, for the person who asked, *"Did not I see thee in the garden with him?"* (John 18:26), was a relative of the man whose ear Peter had just cut off.

As for you, my reader, it has not been long since you were angry when someone blasphemed or spoke a harsh word against one of God's servants or against God's Gospel. I am not sure that it was right for you to be angry, but, at any rate, it was a holy zeal that made you angry. Why, you were red in the face as you defended the truth. I repeat, I am not sure you did well to be angry, but, at any rate, while you were cutting off that man's ear with that sword of yours and dealing out such hard blows for Christ, you certainly appeared to be one of His disciples, even though your Master would not have wanted you to use the sword or to be so violent. Yet your very zeal for Him, though perhaps indiscreet and not altogether what He would approve, showed that you really had some love for Him, some seeking after Him, some zeal for His glory. Is this not so? Surely you also are one of His disciples. These things led people to suspect Peter, and these things lead people to suspect you.

Interest in Jesus

There was something else about Peter as he stood warming his hands by the fire: he was especially interested in the fate of Jesus. Perhaps he tried to avoid showing that he had any particular interest in the trial, but I will guarantee you that those who could read faces could read something in Peter's face as it was lit up by the glare of the coals. When he heard them strike his Master across the face, did you not see that tear fall from Peter's eye? He pretended he was brushing away a drop of sweat from his brow, but anyone who was watching him, especially one with quick eyes, like the maid who spoke, could see that it was a drop of another sort that was falling from his eye.

And when Christ was accused and replied so mildly, or else did not reply at all, you could see a twitching about Peter's mouth. He did not know how to bear it. There was a conflict going on within his spirit. He loved his Master; how could he not love Him? But he was afraid of men, and his face must have looked as though he were agitated by battling storms, as the deep emotions went sweeping over his soul. Those who watched him saw it, though he was not aware of their keen gaze.

Now, you have not said that you are a disciple of Christ, but have others not caught you sometimes by reading it in your face? When you hear a sermon on the Redeemer's sufferings, your soul melts. When others speak of His glories, you exult in the theme. And when the Gospel is preached earnestly to sinners, your eyes look somehow as if you understood it and as if you loved it. Though perhaps you would hardly venture to say, "I am saved," you experience a joy and delight in hearing the truth that you would not know if you were not one of His. You experience a holy trembling and soul-searching when hearing the Word of God that you would not experience unless you were already quickened by the Spirit of His grace.

Yes, the face will often betray what is going on within. Those dear ones who are looking with concern at you, anxious to know whether you are saved, have observed many things about you that have compelled them to cheerfully say, "We believe so-and-so is a Christian. We cannot doubt it. There is something about his whole demeanor, his conversation, his way of thinking, and his way of acting, that betrays him as being a disciple of Christ."

Your Secret Life

Now, beloved friend, I cannot see into your home and judge your secret life, but I will ask you some questions about your private affairs. You have lately put your trust in Christ Jesus alone. If you have not done so, or if you are not sure that you have done so, at any rate you do not have anything else that you are trusting in, and all your trust has been placed on Him. You do see that perfection is unattainable in the flesh, and you are looking for the perfection that Jesus gave to His people when He finished His sacrifice and sat down at the right hand of God. Though you cannot see much light, you know there is no light except in Him, and you are done with that false light that you once rejoiced in. Well, I am glad, and I am inclined to ask you the question, *"Art not thou also one of his disciples?"*

Why, you have recently begun to pray, and not merely as a matter of form. You have stopped using the prayer that you once repeated, and now you pray from your very heart. Sometimes you cannot pray as you would like; in fact, you never do state your petition quite as you desire. Still, you pray as well as you can, with groans and tears and longings that you may be taught how to pray better. Well, I have never heard yet of a praying soul who was not one of Christ's disciples. It was a sign that Saul of Tarsus was a convert to Christ when it was said of him, *"Behold, he prayeth"* (Acts 9:11). And so, I will ask you the question, since you utter the living prayer of a truly earnest soul, "Despite your doubts and questions and humble cries, *'art not thou also one of his disciples?'"*

Moreover, now you have an interest in the Word of God. The Book was very dull to you once; a three-volume novel pleased you much more. Now, anything that will tell you about your Lord and His love, anything that will instruct you in His truth, anything of that sort you enjoy; you hunger for it. Well, I have never known a dead person to become hungry, and I have never heard of a black crow that desired to feed on the food of a dove. I think there must be some change in you, or you would not love the clean, winnowed grain that God's children delight in. I am not sure about it, but still I will venture to ask the question, and I think I know what answer you will give: *"Art not thou also one of his disciples?"*

Besides, you know there is a change in your life. As a child, you are now striving to honor your parents. As a businessman, you have given up many

111

wrong practices. As an acquaintance speaking to others, you are now more charitable in your comments. There are things that were once amusements, that once yielded you pleasure, that have now become *"vanity of vanities"* (Eccl. 1:2) to you. Now, you know that when you rise in the morning, the thing you are most afraid of is that you should do wrong during the day. And if you are troubled at night, it is because you have committed a sin, and the matter that pains you most about it is not the loss of a godly habit, but the loss of a peaceful conscience.

I think that if you are all this, surely you are also one of His disciples. If you are not wholly looking to Him for salvation, but there are such changes in your life as these, surely you also are one of His followers. But it is not mine to answer the question; it is only mine to ask it. One thing I will say, however: either you are His disciple or you are not; that is certain. No one can remain neutral and undecided. *"He that is not with me is against me"* (Matt. 12:30). If you are not Christ's disciple, you are certainly an individual unreconciled to God. Which, then, are you? *"Art not thou also one of his disciples?"*

A Desire to Be Called His Disciple

I have suggested many hopeful things that would lead me to think that you are His disciple, but if you are not, then you are His enemy. What do you think about that? If I should list every believer (supposing I were able to do that) and if this book of believers were just about complete, could you bear that I should say, "I am about to close this book. I have written down all the disciples of Christ here. I have finished the list, and your name is not there"? I am sure you would say, "Oh, wait a minute, sir. I was afraid I was not

112

one of His, but now that it comes right down to it, I do not dare withhold my name." And I am certain that if I were then to take another blank book and begin to write down the names of all those who did not believe in Jesus, those who remained His enemies, if I began to put your name down, you would say, "Oh, no, do not do that. Wait a minute. Do not write down my name. I could not stand that, for I think I am not quite His enemy, surely. At any rate, I long to be His disciple."

Sometimes I wish that you would push yourself into this corner. If it really came to this point, some of you who have said, "I am afraid I do not love Him," because you do not love Him as you ought; some of you who have said, "I am afraid I do not trust Him," because you have some doubts and some fears, would be led by God to trust Him and to rejoice in Him.

I remember a story about a certain martyr who had been condemned to die for Christ. About a week before he died, he was full of great fear and trembling. He was afraid of the fire and was very depressed. His fellow prisoner scolded him and told him that he ought to trust in God, that he should not be dismayed and should not be depressed. When the day came for them to burn together, the poor, weak, trembling man stood at the stake and said before the fire was kindled, "Oh, He has come; He has come; He has come; and He has filled my soul with His presence." He died triumphantly, while the other man who had scolded him for his lack of faith recanted at the last minute and became a traitor to Christ's cause. The Lord will help you if you are right toward Him. Still, I pray that you may be delivered from every question about whether you are His disciple or not.

How Disciples Can Be Inconsistent

Now, having written to those who are doubting their status as disciples, I will, in the second place, demand from those of you who seem to be Christ's disciples an answer to this question: Why are your actions not consistent with those of a disciple of Christ? *"Art not thou also one of his disciples?"*

Refusing Reproach

Why, then, are you not sharing His reproach? Peter stood there warming his hands, looking to his personal comfort. Meanwhile, His Master was a few yards away being despised and rejected, mistreated and struck in the face. If you are one of His disciples, is this the place for you, among the coarse crowd around the fire? Is your proper place not at your Lord's side, to be laughed at as He is, falsely accused as He is, and struck as He is?

So then, I may be writing to some who do love Christ, or are suspected of loving Him, but who have never borne His reproach. Your name is not numbered with any Christian church because, well, it is not a very respectable thing in your circle of friends. You have not professed the truths that you believe because you would become extremely unpopular if you did. You have not said in your household, "I am a Christian," because it is clear to you that your husband might not like it or that your father might not have patience with it. You have slunk into the workplace, and you have hidden your true colors, and you have been comfortable with the ungodly. And when they have uttered harsh things about Christ, you have not liked what they have said, but you have not uttered your disapproval. You chimed in with the ungodly. Your silence gave consent to them.

"Art not thou also one of his disciples," and do you refuse the reproach of Christ? Have you forgotten Moses, who, though he could have been like a king in Egypt, took his place with the poor, despised, enslaved Israelites, *"esteeming the reproach of Christ greater riches than the treasures in Egypt"* (Heb. 11:26)? Can you not take your place with Christ's poor people? Are you ashamed of them because they are not titled and rich, or because their social standing is not very high? Are you ashamed of them because other people misrepresent and slander them?

Has the offense of the Cross ceased? Do you expect that true Christianity will ever be fashionable? Do you believe in your heart for a moment that Christ spoke a lie when He said, *"Behold, I send you forth as sheep in the midst of wolves"* (Matt. 10:16)? If there is a religion about which all men speak well, stay away from it, for it cannot be the religion of Christ. Do you not know that the way to heaven is upstream? The current runs downward to the gulf of destruction. Are you not willing to take the Cross and to go against common opinion and against everything else that you must go against, for Christ's sake?

The day is coming when those who have been ashamed of His Cross will find themselves losing His crown. "No Cross, no crown," the saying goes. "Whoever has been with Me in this evil generation will be with Me when I come in the glory of My Father." That, virtually, is Christ's word to His people. His actual words were, *"Whosoever shall be ashamed of me and of my words, of him shall the Son of man be ashamed"* (Luke 9:26), but, *"Whosoever therefore shall confess me before men, him will I confess also before my Father which is in heaven"* (Matt. 10:32).

If you do not dare to follow Him because you fear shame, shame will be your perpetual inheritance. Remember that verse, *"But the fearful, and unbelieving...shall have their part in the lake which burneth with fire"* (Rev. 21:8). Oh, that we may never be among those cowards, for those are the people He means—not the fearing ones, but the fearful ones, who do not dare to be reproached for Him.

Is there someone reading these words who loves his Lord, knows the truth, and knows where God's church is, yet has been afraid to join His people—ashamed to confess the truth and to follow Christ? I come to you with this word, and I wish I could look you in the face and say, *"Art not thou also one of his disciples?"* Yet you go in and out with the ungodly, and you warm your hands at their fire, and you are happy with their hilarity, and you are pleased with their ungodliness. You must stop this! *"Come out from among them, and be ye separate, saith the Lord, and touch not the unclean thing"* (2 Cor. 6:17). Confess Christ so that He may confess you.

Failing to Witness

If you are among Christ's disciples, why are you not witnessing for Him? Peter not only refused to share His shame, but he did not even speak up for Christ. When Christ was on trial, every person who could have spoken a good word for Him should have done so, for He was worthy. But everyone was silent. When Christ said, *"I spake openly"* (John 18:20), might not Peter have said, "Yes, I have heard all He said. I have never heard Him utter sedition or blasphemy. Nothing of the kind has ever come from my

116

Master's lips. If anything has been spoken in secret, I have been there. I have been with John and James in the most select circle of all His disciples, and so I can bear witness that He is innocent"? But no, Peter was silent, and instead of witnessing he denied his Master.

It is the duty of every Christian to be a witness for Christ. Still, every day, Jesus is on trial. He stands before the world, as it were, at this very hour, and the question is, Is He the Son of God or not? Witnesses are being examined every day for Him and against Him. "What do you think about Christ?" is a question that is stirring all the cities and all the lands, more or less. Now, should He who is the claimant of the royal crown, who claims to be the Savior of men and the head of the church, should He, while so many speak against Him, lack the evidence of anyone who knows Him, who has been with Him and loves Him? Oh, there are some of us who find it sweet to testify that He is the very Christ, and we do not take any honor to ourselves for so doing, for flesh and blood has not revealed it unto us (Matt. 16:17).

Is anyone holding back his testimony? "Why," someone says, "what would my testimony be worth?" You do not know. "Nobody would notice me. I am only a humble woman in my family." What! And do you not have a desire that your family should know the truth? Do you have one little child on your knee, and have you never put your arms around that little one and prayed that she might belong to Jesus, or that he might be the Savior's? Have you never told those darlings of yours what Christ has done for you? You could not do it, you say? Not talk to your own child of what is written in your own heart concerning your own Lord? Ah, if you cannot, then cry to God against such a disability, and do not be satisfied

117

until you have conquered your unholy shame, for unholy it is.

If you also are one of His disciples, bear witness, even if there is only one person to hear it. If that is all the congregation that God sends you, you have done your part. I am not accountable for the number of people who hear, but only for the witness that I bear. You will not be accountable for the largeness or smallness of your sphere, but for the faithfulness of your testimony for Christ. Tell all with whom you come in contact that He is your Savior, a precious Savior, a true Promiser, a Keeper of Promises, a faithful Friend, a Helper in life and in death. I say again, you do not know what may be the value of your testimony, for if it is told only to a child, that child may grow up to bear testimony to tens of thousands. You do not know what may come of a spark of fire. Only let it spark, and you might set half a continent ablaze. *"Art not thou also one of his disciples?"* If you are, then give your testimony in addition to taking up your cross.

Forfeiting Privileges

Now, I want to diverge a little from what some of you would call practical. Let me say, If you are one of His disciples, why are you not enjoying the privileges that belong to His disciples? You have not been baptized, yet He who said, "Believe," also said, "Be baptized" (Matt. 28:19). It is written of some, *"These are they which follow the Lamb whithersoever he goeth"* (Rev. 14:4). I will ask you, Did the Lamb not go down into the Jordan? Was He not baptized? Have you followed Him wherever He has gone? If you have not done so, you have lost a privilege because you have been disobedient to His will.

118

Then there is the Lord's Supper. It is only an outward form just as baptism is—both are only symbols—but still the Lord has been pleased to say, *"This do in remembrance of me"* (Luke 22:19). In the breaking of bread, Christ often gives to His people very sweet manifestations of Himself. You are one of His disciples, or at least I suspect that you are, but you have never been to a Communion service. "There are others who can observe those things," you say. Wait. Suppose it is right for any one Christian to neglect the ordinances of God's house. Clearly, there can be no exceptions; it would, therefore, be right for all Christians to neglect baptism and Communion.

You are not a member of any Christian church, but you think you are right in standing alone. If you are, then all would be, and clearly the visible church would become extinct. But it could never have been the Lord's intention that it should be extinct. He has not ordained that His people should live as individuals alone. He calls Himself a shepherd because sheep stick together. They flock together, and He would have His people do the same. If Christ had called Christians by the name of some other animal, it might be supposed that they would go to heaven separately and alone. But He describes them as sheep of a flock, and that signifies fellowship and union.

Are you right in not participating in baptism and Communion? Are you sure? If you are right, then we would all be right in doing as you do, and where and how could the means of grace be maintained? Would not the very preaching of the Gospel almost become extinct, for the church of God is "the pillar and ground of the truth." I suppose this saying means that as in the Roman forum there were certain pillars upon which the decrees of the senate were hung, so the church is a pillar upon which God hangs the Gospel. The church's proclamation of the Gospel is the pillar upon which God exhibits the Gospel to all onlookers. And truly it must be so. The church's business is to evangelize; the church's business is to maintain ordinances. But where would there be a church to do this if all Christians were allowed to remain separate from the church?

Your business is to find some company of believers, unite yourself with them, and enjoy the church privileges that Christ has given, such as His two ordinances of baptism and the Lord's Supper. In addition, you will enjoy all the other blessings that belong to the church. *"Art not thou also one of his disciples?"* His disciples meet to remember Him, and you turn your back. While they gather at the table, feeding upon the bread and wine that are emblems of Him, you turn away and seem to say, "I do not want these. Christ has instituted an ordinance that I do not need. I can do without it. I am so spiritual that I do not need it." Oh, do not say so. If you are one of His disciples, do as He tells you.

Overlooking His Rest

Let me share a more cheerful thought in closing. *"Art not thou also one of his disciples?"* Then why are you not resting in His love, in His grace, and in His power? You opened this book with a burden upon your spirit that is crushing you into the very dust. You are low and depressed and miserable, and your acquaintances know it, yet they know that you are a professed Christian. *"Art not thou also one of his disciples?"* Your Lord said,

> *Behold the fowls of the air: for they sow not, neither do they reap, nor gather into barns; yet*

*your heavenly Father feedeth them....Consider
the lilies of the field, how they grow; they toil
not, neither do they spin: and yet I say unto
you, That even Solomon in all his glory was
not arrayed like one of these....Therefore take
no thought, saying, What shall we eat? or,
What shall we drink?   (Matt. 6:26, 28–29, 31)*

You also are one of His disciples, yet you are distressing yourself with cares and troubles just like an unbeliever.

Oh, but you have lost a friend, a child, a husband, or a father, and you are crushed into the very dust. You have no hope now, and you are angry with your God. Yet Christ said, *"Not as I will, but as thou wilt"* (Matt. 26:39). *"Art not thou also one of his disciples?"* Are you acting like your Master? He drank the cup of gall, but you shove it away and fight against your God. How can this be? "But I am afraid of an evil that is coming upon me," you say. Has He not said through the apostle Paul, *"Be careful* [anxious] *for nothing; but in every thing by prayer and supplication with thanksgiving let your requests be made known unto God"* (Phil. 4:6)? *"Your heavenly Father knoweth that ye have need of all these things"* (Matt. 6:32), and you are one of His disciples, yet you are fearing the future. Oh, friend! Does this suit you as a Christian? Is this right?

I recently sat at the bedside of a dearly beloved friend to whom I have already referred. Strange as it seems, he had been unconscious for two days, but the moment he heard my voice, he opened his eyes and said, "Oh, how happy I am to see your face once again, my dear pastor!" Then he began to pour out a blessed torrent of adoration and praise to his God. He said that he was barely alive, yet the happiest man alive, and that Christ was more precious than ever. He was rejoicing as he was sinking gently away. He said that he was as happy as he had ever been in his life, and even happier, though there was a rattling in his throat and he could barely breathe.

You are afraid to die, are you? You are a disciple of the blessed Lord who is helping my dear friend to die, and you think that He will not help you, too? Why, thousands of His people have closed their eyes on earth, only to open them in heaven. Thousands have died triumphantly. Thousands have passed through the river of death, sweetly and calmly rejoicing in Him. And you are also one of the disciples of the same Master—the same Master who can

> Make a dying bed,
> Feel soft as downy pillows are.

Your Master has said, *"Fear thou not; for I am with thee: be not dismayed; for I am thy God"* (Isa. 41:10). Yet, you cannot trust Him who has been so faithful to others, and, let me say, who has been so faithful to you up until this very moment. Oh, if you are indeed His disciple, go and put that aching head of yours right on the bosom of your Lord. Within that bosom palpitates a heart that never changes and that never fails one of His disciples. Go and rest there. You may rest, for it is well, it must be well, for the present, for the future, for time, for eternity. If you are one of His disciples, take His yoke upon you, and learn from Him. Like Him, be meek and lowly of heart, and you will find rest for your soul (Matt. 11:29).

Remember, your place is not to question what God does; your place is not to arraign Him in your courtroom. Your duty is not to say, "My will be done," but, *"It is enough for the disciple that he be as his master, and the servant as his lord"* (Matt. 10:25). Your Lord was patient, submissive, acquiescent in the Father's will; and you, His disciple, should follow His example. Walk side by side with your suffering and patient Lord, and may He bless you!

Run No Risk

I do trust that the questions I have asked will not be lost on my readers. You may think that it is not necessary to answer whether you are Christ's disciple or not, but it will be very necessary to answer that question soon. I have been struck beyond measure lately with our mortality, and with the suddenness with which we leave this world. Every now and then I hear from friends—I heard it this last week—"Brother so-and-so walked into my shop on Thursday, and on Sunday I heard that he was dead." "Sister so-and-so was at the Communion service, and within forty-eight hours she died." It is indeed a dying world.

Run no risk of losing your soul—not even the risk of one night. This night, at midnight, without a knock at the door, there might come the messenger who will say, *"Prepare to meet thy God"* (Amos 4:12). And then it will matter whether you are Christ's disciple or not. It will not matter whether you are rich or not, whether you are educated or not. But it will matter for all eternity whether you are His or not, for remember the division that God makes: *"These* [the unrighteous] *shall go away into everlasting punishment: but the righteous into life eternal"* (Matt. 25:46). May God grant that you be among the disciples of Jesus, for Jesus Christ's sake.

Chapter 7

Blessings Traced to Their Source

All my springs are in thee.
—Psalm 87:7

It does us good to think that there are such things in the world as springs bubbling up in shady nooks, places of sweet refreshment on this dusty earth. Our mouths water at the very thought of Elim's twelve wells of water and seventy palm trees (Exod. 15:27). If fresh springs are a blessing even to us, they must have been even more so to the psalmist, who lived in a dry and thirsty land that depended entirely on irrigation. Nothing is more precious to the Oriental than a well, and he who finds a spring considers himself a much happier man than he who finds a vein of precious metal. We must transfer, therefore, the thought of precious water springing up abundantly, bubbling up with living force, to our spiritual condition; then we can say with David, *"All my springs are in thee."* That is, we trace all the mercies we receive to their fountainhead.

The psalmist was grateful for the blessings that were given to him. He did not receive them with selfish inattention, but considering them well, he found that every good gift and every perfect gift came from his God (James 1:17). He had learned that not only everything good around him, but everything good within him, came from the same source. Discovering within his own nature a living power, a living well of water, he traced that also to the grace of God and said, *"All my springs are in thee."*

Was he not referring, first of all, to all the springs from which he drank? Secondly, was he not referring to all the springs that were within himself? I do not know that those two concepts comprise even one-tenth of the thoughts that might arise out of our text, but it would require too many pages to take such a great text as this and consider it in full. I will, therefore, take just these two concepts.

The Springs from Which We Drink

The first thought is, All the springs from which I drink are in You. This brings to mind several different ideas.

The Deep Waters

To begin with, the psalmist might have been thinking of the deep waters that lie under the earth. When Moses blessed the tribes of Israel, he said that Joseph was to have the blessing of *"the deep that coucheth beneath"* (Deut. 33:13). Deep down in the earth are vast reservoirs of water, and when these are tapped, they spring up, and we are refreshed by them.

These are symbolic of the mighty fountains of eternal love, the electing grace of God, and the infinite fullness of the heart of God in His own nature,

for His nature and His name are love. When we get
to the great fountains of the infinite, eternal, immu-
table love of the Father toward His chosen people,
then indeed we come to the fountainhead of all the
streams that *"make glad the city of God"* (Ps. 46:4).
There is not a blessing we receive that cannot be
traced to the eternal purpose of God. We may see, on
every single blessing of the covenant, the stamp of
the eternal purpose and decree. I trace streams of
love up to the Fountain, God,

> And in His mighty breast I see
> Eternal thoughts of love to me.

Every Christian who is properly taught, who
understands the Word of God and is not afraid of the
fullness of the truth, will ascribe all the springs of
grace that he ever drinks of to the eternal fount. Job
said, *"Hast thou entered into the springs of the sea?
or hast thou walked in the search of the depth?"* (Job
38:16). This is a mysterious subject, and we cannot
find these secret springs. Yet, we know that they are
there; we rejoice in them and bless the Lord for
them.

Water from the Rock

However, let us use illustrations from Scripture
to understand what the psalmist meant in our text.
When the psalmist said, "All my fresh springs are in
You," for that is the meaning of the expression he
used, he might have been thinking of the rock that
yielded water in the wilderness. Living water leaped
from the rock so that all the multitude who were in
the desert drank of the stream. Those who had the
true knowledge of God also drank from the spiritual

Rock that followed them, and we know that that Rock was Christ (1 Cor. 10:4). Even as the rock in the wilderness was struck and immediately became a spring of water for all the Israelite tribes, so our smitten Savior has now become the spring from which all of us drink. So I may say,

> Rock of Ages, cleft for me,
> Thou my sacred fount shalt be.

We find, pouring from the cleft in His side, both the cleansing blood and the refreshing water. Even as I said before that we may trace all our blessings to electing love, so I now say with equal truthfulness that we may trace them all to redeeming love. There is a crimson mark on every blessing of the covenant. You see on all the favors that God sends to us the mark of the pierced hand:

> There's ne'er a gift His hand bestows
> But cost His heart a groan.

That is a sure and precious truth. As we look to our dear Lord upon the cross, as we see Him exalted in His glory, we remember that *"it pleased the Father that in him should all fulness dwell"* (Col. 1:19), and, *"of his fulness have all we received, and grace for grace"* (John 1:16). We can truly say to Him, "Emmanuel, *'all my springs are in thee.'"*

Controversial Waters

We see in the Holy Scriptures another illustration. During the time of Abraham, there were certain wells that he dug, the possession of which was disputed by the Philistines. Later on, when Isaac had to go into Philistia, he found that the wells that Abraham had dug had been stopped up by the Philistines. Therefore, he dug others, and the Philistines began to quarrel with his herdsman. Being a peaceful man, he moved on a few miles farther and dug another well, but the Philistines argued over that one, too. It seemed as if he could have no water without having to contend for it.

Sometimes the wells from which we drink are springs about which there is serious contention. There are some who deny the most precious doctrines of the Gospel. Archers are waiting at the well, and when a poor, simple child of God comes and lets down his bucket to get a drink, he finds the bowman's arrow going past his ear. Somebody has decided that one doctrine is not scriptural, that another doctrine is not rational, so the thirsty soul becomes afraid to drink from that well.

What is worse, if there is not a controversy about the truth itself, the child of God finds a controversy in his own soul as to his right to use it. Satan, *"the accuser of our brethren"* (Rev. 12:10), will remind him of his faults, will tell him he has no part in the matter or else he would not be what he is. But *"they that are delivered from the noise of archers in the places of drawing water"* (Judg. 5:11) will bless the name of the Lord as they drink.

Beloved, remember at all times that all our mercies come from God. Regardless of what logic may insist on, it must be true that *"salvation is of the LORD"* (Jonah 2:9). Whichever "ism" might be right, whichever side of a controversy might have made an accurate statement, it must be correct that every good thing comes from *"the Father of lights, with whom is no variableness, neither shadow of turning"* (James 1:17). If we remember these things, we will find that, let the Enemy argue as he will, we have access to the refreshing stream.

Since all the springs worth drinking from are in God our Father and Christ our Redeemer, we can come to these and drink without fear; for God is ours, and Christ is ours, and therefore every covenant blessing is ours, too. Therefore, laying aside all disputing and contention, we come and drink from these wells because they are in God and in Christ our Savior.

The Upper Springs and Lower Springs

In the book of Judges, we read about two springs of water—*"the upper springs and the nether* [lower] *springs"* (Judg. 1:15). Now, every child of God who judges correctly knows that his lower springs are in God. By his lower springs, I mean his lower comforts, his temporal mercies. What would we have on this earth worth enjoying if God did not give it to us? If you have wealth, who gave you power to get it? And if you have health, who is it that preserves the strength of your body, and the blood that flows within your veins? God has only to will it, and you would be a paralytic. If your children are spared, bless God for each of them, for it is He who spares them. Your husband or your wife, your brother or your friend, the joys that you enjoy in your home— all these come to you through Him. They are common mercies, we say, but we would not think of them as so common if they were gone for a while. Let us bless God and see His hand and say, "Great Father, even my lower springs are in You."

Regarding the upper springs, there is no question. If we possess eternal life, God gave it to us. If we believe in Jesus, it is because of God, for faith is not a flower that springs from the natural soil of

man's heart. If we have repented and gained eternal
life, it is the work of the Spirit of God. If we have
remained faithful to our profession of faith, we have
nothing to boast about; we would have gone back
from it if God had not preserved us. We have never
had one single bit of anything that we did not receive from the Lord's infinite mercy. All our upper
springs are in Him. Should we not bless His name?
While we say, *"Spring up, O well"* (Num. 21:17),
should we not also add, *"Sing ye unto it"* (v. 17)?
Bless and magnify that perennial fount of mercy
that perpetually flows to us.

For inspiration, the classical poets went to
Mount Helicon, the home of the Muses in Greek my-
thology. But, as for us, we will say with that poet of
the sanctuary,

> Come, thou fount of every blessing,
> Tune my heart to sing Thy praise.
> Streams of mercy never ceasing
> Call for songs of loudest praise.

We have no Helicon, but we have a better mount:

> Teach me some melodious sonnet,
> Sung by flaming tongues above:
> Praise the mount—oh fix me on it,
> Mount of God's unchanging love.

From this source we will derive our inspiration; here
we will find our song. The upper and the lower
springs come alike from God.

Springs in the Valleys

In Psalm 104 we read of the springs in the valleys (v. 10). Valleys are the places for springs. Wild

beasts come to drink there, and each one of them quenches its thirst (v. 11). In the valleys, the birds sing among the branches (v. 12). You and I have had our valley mercies. We have been humiliated, perhaps, and we have sung,

> He that is down need fear no fall,
> He that is low no pride.
> He that is humble ever shall
> Have God to be his Guide.

We have been in the valley of Baca and have made it a well, and the rain has filled the pools (Ps. 84:6). We have been in the valley of fellowship with Christ, walking along in the cool vale of communion with our Father who is in heaven, and, behold, it has been the place of springs—of springs full of water. There is not one joy in our best and happiest time that does not come from God. In our choicest moments, when we are fullest of the Lord and freest from the encumbrances of the earth, never, even then, do we have anything that is from ourselves. If it is good, it comes from God.

Streams in the Desert

Then, we read in Isaiah, and also in some other biblical passages, of the streams in the desert. *"In the wilderness shall waters break out, and streams in the desert"* (Isa. 35:6). *"I will open rivers in high places"* (Isa. 41:18). That is an odd place for rivers. *"I will open rivers in high places, and fountains in the midst of the valleys: I will make the wilderness a pool of water, and the dry land springs of water"* (v. 18).

Do you remember your dryland springs? Can you not remember when you ate of treasures hidden in the sand; when it was dark and yet never so light; when you were in the land of barrenness and yet never were so filled with plenty; when you had abounding troubles and yet never had such super-abundant comforts? Oh, let us bless the Lord that our desert springs were in Him. They were in Him, or we would not have had them. If the Lord had not been with us, we would have fallen and died in the wilderness like those who came out of Egypt, whose dead bodies covered the plain.

Pisgah Springs

In the fourth chapter of Deuteronomy, we find springs that some of God's saints drink from that are not often mentioned—the Pisgah springs (v. 49). In this chapter, Moses was speaking of the springs that came from the foot of a mountain called Pisgah—where he stood to view the Promised Land. Believe me, they are cool streams indeed; a drink from them *"goeth down sweetly, causing the lips of those that are asleep to speak"* (Song 7:9). He who knows what heaven is and has by faith looked it over, who has seen its security, its purity, its nearness to God, its revelation of the face of Christ, its communion of saints, its joy of the Lord—such a one has found the Pisgah springs to be very precious and very soul-reviving. Oh, for a drink of them now! I take a drink of them when I sing that hymn,

A scrip on my back, and a staff in my hand,
  I march on in haste through an enemy's land;
The way may be rough, but it cannot be long,
  And I'll smooth it with hope, and cheer it with song.

The prospect of the coming glory makes the Pisgah springs well up, and all of them are in our God, for there would be no hope of heaven without Him. There would be banishment into eternal woe if it were not for His infinite grace.

If I were to continue to use illustrations from Scripture, I could show that whatever sort of springs there may be, all of them come from the great depths of the infinite love of God. All our springs are in Him.

The Springs That Are within Us

Now we come to our other subject, namely, that all the springs that are within us come from the same source. You know our Savior's promise to the person who drinks of the water that He gives. It *"shall be in him a well of water springing up into everlasting life"* (John 4:14).

A Christian is not a pitcher that is filled and emptied. He is simply a receiver, a reservoir. By God's grace he becomes a living well. He is not a puppet moved with strings; he is not a machine that is wound up and moves mechanically. There is a living power in him! He is a new creation in Christ Jesus (2 Cor. 5:17), prompted by the highest form of life, and he possesses that life in the highest degree of freedom. While a man is a free agent before he is converted, he is in a far superior sense a free agent when he becomes a converted soul. *"If the Son therefore shall make you free, ye shall be free indeed"* (John 8:36).

The Springs of the Inner Life

Our text, then, might mean that all the springs of my inner life, if I possess them, lie in God. *"For ye are dead, and your life is hid with Christ in God"*

(Col. 3:3). *"And you hath he quickened, who were dead in trespasses and sins"* (Eph. 2:1). Christ is your life. All the springs of life are in Him.

In addition, all the springs of our secret thoughts and of our devotion are in Him. You cannot think of God and worship God to the same degree at all times. If you can, and it is real devotion, I greatly envy you. I find in my soul that there are times when I have the wings of an eagle. I can mount up and, with unblinking eye, look into the infinite glory. There are times when I can soar on and on in strange ecstasy and delight. But, at other times, I cannot rise from the ground. The chariot wheels have been taken off, as in Pharaoh's case (Exod. 14:24-25), so that I drag heavily. In these times, Dr. Watt's hymn seems appropriate:

> Our souls can neither fly, nor go
> To reach eternal joys.

It seems that the preacher is sometimes fertile enough, and at other times he is barren. Truly, the Christian experience is like Pharaoh's dream. He saw lean cows and fat cows, withered ears of corn and good ears of corn (Gen. 41:17-24). There is undoubtedly a lesson in this for the Christian: when he has sacred thoughts and devotion, they come from God, but he is sometimes left on his own to learn of his own emptiness. To show that the strength of Samson did not lie in muscle and tendon and bone alone, Samson's hair was shaved off. He went out as before, but could perform no feat of strength. He was as weak as any other man. Yes, beloved, if we have any power of thought, any sweetness of devotion, or any drawing near to God, all the springs lie in Him.

This concept is most certainly true regarding the springs of our emotions. Do you not find yourself sometimes sweetly melted down by the power of God's Word? Could you not at such times sit and weep over the thought of the death of Jesus and His unspeakable love for you? Do you not sometimes feel stirred with sacred joy, so that you could burst out with an impromptu "hallelujah," or begin to sing a new song about His great love? At other times you think about the same theme, but your heart does not feel it. Exactly the same song is sung, but though your lips join in, your heart does not join in with the music. You know it is so.

You cannot command your own spirit; the Lord must help you. The springs of your emotions lie in His hand. If He leaves you, you are like the Arctic Ocean—freezing. But when He comes and smiles at you, all the icebergs melt in a moment, and your heart feels the warm Gulf Stream of eternal love flowing right through it. Then comes the blossoming of spring and the singing of birds; your whole heart is alive to the Most High. The springs of your devotion, as well as your sacred thoughts, all lie in Him.

The Springs of All True Actions

I am sure that the springs of all true actions lie in God. Christians are not all thought and all emotion; they are practical people who work for God. But has one of us ever done a good work in his own strength? We have done many works in our own strength, but were they good for anything? The Savior will decide that question. He says, *"Without me ye can do nothing"* (John 15:5). You can bring forth fruit without Him, but it is like fruit from the vine of Sodom and from the fields of Gomorrah (Deut. 32:32). Only that which comes from Him is truly good. When He blesses us, the actions that we do for Him are accepted through Him.

Well, beloved, it will always be true that our springs of holy zeal, our springs of joy, our springs of fellowship, our springs of every kind that are worth having, all lie in Him. It will be good if the church recognizes that. We cannot drum up a revival; it is a great pity that we should ever try. Such a revival, if we seem to get it, will be very harmful. But the Lord can send us a true revival.

All our springs are in Him. We must not depend on ministers and say, "If so-and-so preaches, there will be good results." Our springs are not in these poor wells called ministers; they are in our God. When will the church turn her eyes from the creature to the Creator? When will she purge herself of that hereditary fault of digging cisterns for herself— broken cisterns—and forgetting the fountains of living waters (Jer. 2:13)? I am persuaded from my own experience that the more I live upon God alone, the more I truly live. The less I know of my own so-called power, or wisdom, or grace, or anything of the sort, the better. The more I decrease and He increases, the more I grow up in the Lord in all things. May we, then, adopt this sweet motto: "All my springs that are within me, as well as those from which I drink, are in my God."

Practical Lessons

We should apply this precious text to our lives. We can do this in three ways.

First, let us look to these springs. If you do not think that you measure up, if you are dull and heavy and have no springs in yourself, remember that they were never there. *"All my springs are in thee."* Do you feel empty? Well, you only feel as you always are. Do you feel as though death were written upon you? It is quite true; it is. But your life is in Christ. Your fullness is in Christ. Your strength is in Christ.

Has someone told you that Christ has lost His power, that His life has declined? If so, you have great cause for weeping indeed. But while He is the same, the well of water is the same. Perhaps you feel like Hagar; every drop of water in the bottle is gone. Well, it never was much of a bottle, and it leaks. Now, you think, "What will I do? All my little supply is gone." *"What aileth thee, Hagar?"* (Gen. 21:17). There is a well near you. Open your eyes, for God sees you, and God provides for you. Christ is the same. "Oh, but I think I have forgotten Him," you say. Remember Him, then. "But I fear that I am not one of His people." Well, if you are not a saint, you are a sinner, and He came to save sinners.

I always find a quick reply to the Devil to be the best kind. "Oh," he says, "you are no child of God." "No," I say to him, "and neither are you." "Ah," he says, "but you have no true experience." "No," I say, "I do not. You do not, either. But one thing I know: I am sinful, and Christ has said that I will be made clean by washing in His blood by faith. If I cannot go to Him as a saint, I will go even now as a sinner. If I have been mistaken in the past about my salvation, I will begin again." Child of God, that is the only way to end the controversy. Go and stand at the foot of the cross again. Begin again, for all your springs are still there. Though you cannot find any springs in yourself, they are still in God.

Let Your Streams Flow to God

The next way to apply our text is this: if all my springs are in God, then I must let all my streams flow to God. All the rivers run into the sea because they all came from the sea. It is from the sea that the sun forms the clouds, which feed the thousand brooks, which fall into the rivers, which run back to the sea. Let us do the same. What we have had from God must go back to God. Even in the temporary things of this life, we ought to do this.

I remember a story that Martin Luther told. When certain monks complained that the income of the monastery had gotten very low, he said, "It is no wonder. At one time, we used to entertain two strangers at the monastery, the one named 'Give,' the other named 'It Shall Be Given.' Now, you threw out Give, and very soon God took away It Shall Be Given, for they are brothers, and they live together. If you want to have It Shall Be Given, you must take back Give."

When we are not serving God acceptably and consecrating our supplies to God, we lose supplies from God. In temporary things, I have known men to give to God by the shovelfuls, and God sent them wagonloads by the back door. They could not give out their substance as fast as He sent it in. He has said, *"Give, and it shall be given unto you; good measure...running over"* (Luke 6:38), and many have found it so. Some mean misers go on hoarding until they die, and have hardly enough to be buried with respectably, while others give liberally and yet grow richer. If our springs are in Him even in temporary things, let the streams run back to Him. Let us not rob God. (See Malachi 3:8.)

And, as to spiritual things, let us give back to God the love He gives us, the faith He gives us, the spiritual strength He gives us. Let us use for Him the experience He has given us, the instruction He has given us. Let us instruct and encourage others to His glory with what we ourselves have received. Let us use every talent and keep none buried in the earth. May the Lord grant that we may always say to Him that, as all our springs are in Him, all our streams will run to Him.

Have Hope in God concerning the Lost

Lastly, in applying our text, let us have a great deal of hope about other people. If all streams are in God, I do not have to consider what is in my fellowmen when I go forth to do good to them. I have to consider what is in God. When I address a sinner and say, "Believe on the Lord Jesus Christ," if I do that because I have a notion that the man can believe, I am making a very gross mistake. If I do it because God tells me to do it, I am doing it for the right reason. I must speak the Gospel message just as I would have said to the dry bones, "Live," being perfectly sure they could not live of themselves. (See Ezekiel 37:1–10.) Then I am doing right, for I am exercising my own faith. It is an act of faith on the preacher's part, and God will bless that act of faith. Many of the dry bones will live; in other words, sinners will believe and will repent.

We must not put our hopes in what is in the sinner. I once heard a man preach on adapting the Gospel to suit the sinner. I thought he was a mighty fool, for what is in the sinner except everything that is opposed to the Gospel, everything that is incompatible, everything that would put the Gospel to death if it could? All the power of the Gospel lies in itself, not in the sinner. Salvation comes from God and God alone. Therefore, there is no reason that I should not preach the Gospel with a hope of success in a prison or in the lowest slums. To those who have sunk as low as the prostitute and the thief, the Gospel comes with a strange newness and often yields fruit.

It was so in the Savior's days. The Pharisees, who knew so much, rejected His word, but the tax collectors and prostitutes entered into the kingdom of heaven before them. If I were commanded by God to preach the Gospel in hell, I would be safe enough to preach it there. I believe it would be effective for salvation there, as far as the characters of persons were concerned, if it were God's will that it should be so.

Therefore, there is nothing about the sinner that we need to tremble about, because if he is dead, God can lift him up. Yes, if he is like Lazarus, dead and buried, the voice of God can call him forth from the tomb. Yes, if he were as nothing, God makes mighty the *"things which are not, to bring to nought things that are"* (1 Cor. 1:28). God can bless where all was cursed. Out of the stones of the brook, He can raise up children to Abraham (Matt. 3:9). Let us have great comfort next Sunday when we preach in church or teach in Sunday school or are used in some other way. All the springs lie in God, and if we work in a dry and thirsty land where there is no water, never mind. Our springs are in God. Our faith is in Him, and *"according to your faith be it unto you"* (Matt. 9:29).

Chapter 8

The Places Where God Blesses

And he blessed him there.
—*Genesis 32:29*

In Genesis 32 is the remarkable account of Jacob wrestling with the angel. Jacob said to the angel, *"Tell me, I pray thee, thy name"* (v. 29). He got no answer to that question; in fact, he was gently rebuked. The angel did not come to gratify Jacob's curiosity, but he came as a messenger from God with a blessing. *"And he blessed him there."*

There are a great many things we would like to know when we read the Bible, but if we read it in order to find salvation, that will be much better than having our curiosity gratified. When we hear a sermon, we would like, perhaps, to hear some fine passages or to hear some interesting anecdotes that we could carry away with us. But if, instead, the Lord's messenger gives us a blessing from God Himself, it is infinitely better. The disciples wanted to know from the Savior something about the times and the seasons in which God would work, but He did not tell it to them. Instead, He told them that they would be filled with the Spirit not many days from then (Acts 1:6–8). That was far better and far more valuable to them. Although at the time it might not have pleased them very much, for all practical purposes it enriched them far more. Angels' names we can afford to do without, but God's blessing we must have; we cannot do without it. *"He blessed him there."*

Let us just think for a minute or two about what this blessing was that Jacob gained as the result of a night of prayer. Have you ever spent a night in prayer? Do you know anyone who has ever wrestled with the angel for so long? I am afraid the answer is probably no. Beloved, it is not easy to continue for a night in prayer. It has been well observed that it is easier to hear a sermon two hours long than to pray for an hour. The more spiritual the exercise, the sooner we tire. Joshua was not weary of fighting in the valley, but Moses' hands began to grow weary with holding them up in prayer. Yet, surely there have been times of hardship in our lives, as in that of Jacob, when a night of prayer would have been fitting. Surely we have been in as dire straits and struggles as he, and surely we have needed the blessing of heaven as much as that tried patriarch. Perhaps it would be wise before long to try this great feat and wait from sunset to sunrise with God.

The knights of old, before they took a higher degree of knighthood, spent a night in some church and were supposed to be in prayer. He who will spend a night in prayer will win celestial blessings. He will lie down a Jacob, but he will rise up a prince. There is distinct progress in going from the name *Jacob,* which means "supplanter," to the name *Israel,* which means "prince." Prayer gives an incalculable blessing. And this is the advance Jacob gained, an incomparable advance in spiritual things.

Besides that, he gained, as the blessing attending that night's prayer, deliverance out of great peril. He thought that he and his would be slain by Esau, but the angel blessed him. Not a single lamb of all his flock was hurt; nor were the women and children frightened by the slightest alarm. Prayer brought down heaven's shield to cover Jacob in the hour of danger.

Again, he got what was better still in some ways: reconciliation with his brother. He had grievously wronged his brother, but his brother forgave him. I do not know for certain, but I think a Christian would almost sooner be exposed to peril than live under a sense of having committed an injustice. It is a great relief to a person's mind to see his wrongs set right again. "I wronged that man, but my sin is gone and forgiven forever" is a blessing worth praying all night to obtain.

Jacob was happy to experience the healing of his relationship with his brother, to meet him and hug him, to feel that, being such near relatives, they should no longer be divided in heart. Are you divided from your brother? Has any root of bitterness sprung up to trouble you (Heb. 12:15)? Have the friendships of life been spoiled by dislike? It would be good to have a night of prayer to get those relationships right again and to again serve side by side. I consider it a vast blessing to a Christian to be delivered from the temptation to retaliate, to be saved from all hardness of heart and bitterness of spirit. When the angel gave Jacob that blessing, he blessed him indeed.

Besides all these blessings—rising in rank before God, having his wrong amended, being forgiven by his brother, being restored to friendship—I do not doubt that from that night a special blessing rested on Jacob's heart. The dews of that night fertilized his soul for years to come. He was anointed with fresh oil from that moment, and as he rose, limping because of his hip, he was not merely a better man by title, but better by nature. He had been in a far-off country with his uncle Laban, and much of the dew had evaporated. However, now that he was returning to Canaan, the angel sealed his return by blessing him. Such were the blessings of Jacob.

I would not be surprised if you, my reader, have said, "I personally know what those blessings are, in a measure, but I wish I enjoyed them fully." My prayer, beloved, is that even now God may bless you. According to your necessity, may He shape the blessing. Oh, may He bless you indeed and bless you now.

In this chapter, I want to answer the following questions: Where did Jacob get his blessing? Are there not other such places? And, lastly, might your life not be one of them?

The Place Where Jacob Received a Blessing

First, then, where did Jacob get his blessing, this choice blessing?

A Place of Trial

It was a place of trial, very severe trial. Jacob had just gotten out of Laban's clutches, only to fall into the path of Esau. He had fled from a lion, and now a bear met him. He feared that his wives and children would be completely destroyed by his revengeful brother. It was a fearful trial, and the mere fear of it must have left scars on his heart. Yet, the angel *blessed him there.* Is this not a very common circumstance with the people of God, that their severest trials are the places of their choicest mercies? I want to remind you how often this has been the case, how Cowper's words have been true:

> The clouds ye so much dread
> Are big with mercies, and shall break
> In blessings on your head.

Believe these words for the trial you are now entering. *"He blessed him there,"* where He tried him. He will bless you there, where He is trying you, in the furnace where he is refining you again and again by heaping hot coals upon you. He will bless you there. The disciples feared, we are told, as they entered into the cloud, but it was during this incident that they saw the Savior transfigured (Matt. 17:1–8). Often we fear the cloud into which we are entering, when we are only coming into the secret place of the Most High, where, under the shadow of the Almighty, we will have even more delightful visions of Him.

If we were wise, we would begin to welcome trials. We should fear to be without them instead of fearing to be with them. What do we not owe to the furnace, to the rod, to the threshing flail? Scarcely has any mercy of any great spiritual value come to us except by way of the cross. I am sure I can look upon every choice blessing I have enjoyed as having come to me in rumbling wagons like the good things that came from Egypt to Jacob in his older years (Gen. 45:21–23). We have been blessed in places of trial. Let us not, therefore, dread to go to such places again, but let us go on our way toward heaven, feeling that whatever difficulty we meet with will only be another place in which God will bless us. *"He blessed him there."*

Jacob's place of blessing was also a place of pleading. That is something to make note of. *"He blessed him there,"* where he spent a night in prayer, where he began a wrestling match with a stranger, where he would not let the stranger go, where he held him fast until he gained the blessing. *"He blessed him there."* If you are short on blessings, resort to the place of mighty prayer. All things are open to the person who knows how to pray persistently. *"The kingdom of heaven suffereth violence, and the violent take it by force"* (Matt. 11:12). Jacob's wrestling was no child's play. Painters have attempted to depict it, and only now and then have they captured the idea. No doubt the angel taxed Jacob's strength to the utmost until, in the dead of night, he was faint, faint with the toil he had gone through.

Begging is hard work. It is said of begging that it is the worst trade in the world, but the man who is going to make anything of prayer must throw his whole soul into it. Your prayers that hardly have enough life in them to live, your words that hang like icicles on your lips, your requests that are scarcely heard by yourself, how do you think they will be heard by God? If there is not enough prayer in us to stir our own hearts, how can we expect God to be moved by our entreaties? If you want a blessing, you must go the way that Jacob went. When you reach the point where you will take no denial, where you would sooner die than not be blessed, you will get the blessing, for *"he blessed him there."*

A Place of Communion

In addition to its being a place of trial and a place of pleading, it was a place of communion. Jacob called it *"Peniel"* (Gen. 32:30), or "the face," because there he had seen God face to face. Oh, beloved, these are things to feel rather than to speak about. To see God! Blessed indeed are the pure in heart when they get this blessing (Matt. 5:8). What a wonderful thing to be so united with Christ as to be able to look to God with an eye that is not blinded with fear. Oh, to speak with God, pouring out our hearts before Him, and to hear Him speaking with us. Then the promise no longer lies like a dead letter on the page, but it leaps out of the page, as though alive, as though God had just spoken it and we were hearing it from His divine mouth.

Do you understand God's Word? Can you read Song of Solomon and say, "I understand it"? Have you ever fed on the body and blood of Christ, having His very life in you? If you have, then you have seen God, and it will be said of you, *"he blessed him there."* Beloved, we miss a thousand blessings because we are too busy to commune with God. We are here, there, and everywhere, except where we ought to be. We are running to this and to that, instead of sitting with Mary at the Master's feet. He blessed Mary as she sat there, and there, too, He will be sure to bless us.

A Place of Conscious Weakness

Jacob got the blessing in a place of conscious weakness. The angel touched the socket of Jacob's hip near the tendon. When he got the blessing, he got lameness, too, and he was likely well content to carry that lameness to his grave. The place where I have seen my own insignificance, lowness, unbelief, and depravity has been the place where I have gotten a blessing.

147

Have you ever tried to preach and failed in the attempt, and have you not found that God blessed you there? Have you ever tried to be earnest with the Sunday school children, but in your own judgment made a fool of yourself? Have you not found that God blessed you there? Is it not often one of the greatest blessings that can happen to us to be made to think little of ourselves? May God not be enriching us the most when He is emptying us? May He not be preparing us for the largest possible blessing when He is causing us to see the completeness of our poverty?

The most unpleasant places to us in life are often the places where the blessing comes the most. *"He blessed him there."* God has taken the rich man from his palace and has made him live in a cottage, but *"he* [has] *blessed him there."* He has taken the strong man's vigor and has laid him on a sickbed, but *"he* [has] *blessed him there."* God has brought down the man full of assurance into a state of trembling and anxiety, but *"he* [has] *blessed him there."* He has brought the man of busy usefulness to the place of being a patient sufferer, unable to stir hand or foot for the Lord he loves so well, but *"he* [has] *blessed him there."* He has taken the man of good reputation and has allowed his character to be maligned and his good name to be slandered, but *"he* [has] *blessed him there."* Oh, it is often so. We limp with lameness, with the taking away of the precious thing in which our strength seemed to lie, but our lameness may be the very means to a blessing that otherwise we would never receive.

I would encourage you, then, to seek a blessing. Most likely you have been in the house of trial. Get a blessing there. The place of pleading, at any rate, is open to you. Get a blessing there. The sacred place of communion is also the place to get a blessing. And I suppose you have had your times of being humbled and of getting very low. Oh, may you get a blessing there.

Others Places of Blessing

There are other places where Christians get blessings besides the place where Jacob won his.

From Eternity

Beloved, there is a place—how should I speak of it?—where the Lord blessed us. That place is eternity. God is so happy to bless His people that He began early. He began before time began. He *"hath blessed us with all spiritual blessings in heavenly places in Christ: according as he hath chosen us in him before the foundation of the world"* (Eph. 1:3–4). When the decree was given, when the covenant was established, when the election was determined, He blessed each one of us there, if indeed we are believers in Jesus.

At the Cross

I could point to a thousand places all down the line of history where all of us in Christ were blessed. But I will only linger at the Cross and say that where Jehovah was made a curse for us and suffered in our place, He blessed us there. And at that open, empty tomb, from which escaped the living Savior, whom the chains of death could not hold, He blessed us there. He who died for our transgression rose again for our justification, and by His resurrection blessed us there. And when, standing on the Mount of Olives about to depart, he pronounced the blessing upon His disciples, He blessed us there.

And as He ascended on high, leading captivity captive, from His royal chariot He lavishly gave ten thousand gifts for the sons of men, which He had received even for the rebellious, so that the Lord God might dwell among them (Ps. 68:18). He blessed us there. And up in heaven, where He sits until His work is done, He points to His wounds and points to our names and reminds the Father of His love for us. He has blessed us there, for He *"hath raised us up together, and made us sit together in heavenly places in Christ Jesus"* (Eph. 2:6). He blessed us there.

In Our Own Experiences

There are places in your own experience, beloved, where He has blessed you. I would like to take you back in your history to the moment that you first knew the Lord. I do not think that you can be reminded of that moment too often. Where was the place in which you were burdened with cares and sins, in which you saw Jesus Christ and looked to Him and at once were set free? Where was it? When was it? Twenty years ago, perhaps; perhaps only two or three years ago; perhaps only a week ago. Well, whenever it was, when God led you to see the Savior, He blessed you there as you had never been blessed before. I would not be surprised if the day were marked down in your diary, though there is little need that it should be, for it is marked forever in your memory. Oh, blessed place, oh, happy moment, when Jesus first met with me! He blessed me there.

Well, since that time, have there not been other places where He has blessed you? If you could think of every trial you have ever had, you could say, "He blessed me there." If you could mention every benefit you have ever received, you could say, "He blessed me there." But time would fail. I will just remind you that when you have been prompt to obey your Lord and keep close to Him, when you have not allowed any cloud to come between you and Him, He has blessed you there. If you have kept up that spirit of obedience, take care to still let your eyes look to Him as the eyes of a maid look to her mistress, for He will bless you there.

Have you not found that when you have been most empty and have had the least self-reliance, He has blessed you there? When you have been very weak and little in your own eyes and ready to die, when you have felt that you were nothing and even less than nothing, has He not blessed you there? When you have stayed low, without an ambitious thought, down on the very ground before Him, and have been afraid to look up because of your sense of unworthiness, has He not blessed you there? Oh, keep to the low places, then. There is no place like the valley of humiliation.

> He that is down need fear no fall,
> He that is low no pride.

It would be difficult for me to say where He has not blessed me. Wherever He has led, wherever He has directed me, if I have sought His blessing, I have found it. Therefore, I will testify to His faithfulness.

Well, by and by, when your time comes to die, He will bless you there. Before that time, you may have to suffer, but He will bless you there. You may lose the dear husband who is now your strength, or the beloved wife who is now your comfort, but He will bless you there. You may have to go to the graveside of one child after another, and you yourself may be very weak and scarcely have life within you, but He will bless you there. What He has been, He will be. If God were changeable, we might doubt, but He never changes. Let us look back through the many days since we first met Him and He met us. Let us remember that we have been upheld until now, and He has helped us in every need.

> After so much mercy past,
> Will He let us sink at last?

What I am saying is very commonplace, and it might have already suggested itself to you. But at the same time, when we get into trouble, it does not suggest itself, and we need to be reminded of these simple principles. He has blessed you in your place of trial, and in such a place He will bless you again.

At Church

Let me say one more thing on this subject. Has He not often blessed you in the house of prayer? Has He not blessed you in listening to the Gospel? I know He has. Never, therefore, neglect the house of God. Has He not blessed you at the prayer meeting? Can you not say, "He blessed me there"? Well, let others see your face there as often as possible. Has He not blessed you at the Communion table? Oh, if there is an ordinance under heaven that is Christ's mirror, if there is a hand under heaven that can draw back the blind and push up the window and let us see the King in His beauty, it is the Lord's Supper. He blesses us there. Let those who despise the Lord's Table stay away, but those who have received the blessing will want to be there often. They will want to come again and again, saying, *"We would see Jesus"* (John 12:21). He blesses us there.

You Can Receive a Blessing

Perhaps you are reading about these blessings and know that you have not been a recipient of them because you are not saved. Are you saying, "I wish God would bless me, even me"? Are you willing, if God helps you, to give up all your sins? Do you want to be clean of them and clear of them? Well, soul, if you desire that, God will bless you now. God wants you to be rid of sin, and if you want to be rid of sin, you and He are agreed. He will be sure to blot out your sins and tread them under His feet through His dear Son Jesus Christ.

Do you want a blessing? I will ask you another question. Are you willing to have Jesus Christ be your Savior, not in part, but altogether? Will you let Christ be the first and the last? Will you take Him, not to be a small part of your life, but to be a Savior who can save you from head to foot, who can give His blood to cleanse you, His righteousness to cover you, Himself to be all in all to you? Soul, if you will take a whole Christ, He waits to be received by you. Only trust Him, and He is yours. *"As many as received him, to them gave he power to become the sons of God"* (John 1:12).

There was once a soul who wanted Christ, *"and he blessed him there."* There was once a soul who wanted to be rid of sin, *"and he blessed him there."* There was once a soul who said, "Lord, save me, or I will perish," *"and he blessed him there."* There was once another soul who said, *"God be merciful to me a sinner"* (Luke 18:13), *"and he blessed him there."* There was once someone who cried to God, and He did not seem to hear, and at last she went through the crowd and touched His garment's hem, *"and he blessed [her] there."* There was once another woman

153

whom He called a dog. She said, *"Yet the dogs eat of the crumbs which fall from their masters' table"* (Matt. 15:27), *"and he blessed* [her] *there."* Oh, anxious, seeking, timid, trembling soul, do trust in Jesus. Rest in Jesus, and He will bless you now, and you will go on your way rejoicing.

You may be a Christian who is in trouble. Brother, sister, I do not know what your trouble is, but there is a little text I would like to share with you: *"Casting all your care upon him; for he careth for you"* (1 Pet. 5:7). Will you not trust in Him after reading that? If you will, He will bless you there. Are you troubled by some need of temporary things? Let me put this into your mouth as a sweet morsel: *"Your Father knoweth what things ye have need of, before ye ask him"* (Matt. 6:8). Savor that, and He will bless you there. Oh, what a blessing will come out of the richness of that thought!

You may be a Christian who is saying, "I feel half ashamed to go to the Communion table; I am so unworthy." Turn your eyes again to the Cross. Look to the Savior for worthiness. You never were worthy, and never will be. He will bless you there. Perhaps you are saying, "I feel so cold and insensitive." Think of the Savior's love for poor, dead, cold sinners such as you are, and He will bless you there. If you are cold, it is no use thinking of the cold in order to get hot; the best thing is to go to the fire. And if you feel dull and dead, do not try to get better by examining yourself. Hurry away to Jesus Christ, and He will bless you there. Let us now say, "Dear Lord, meet with us. Show us Your hands and Your side." If we come to His throne in that spirit of desire, He will bless us there.

May the Lord be with us all, for Jesus' sake.

Chapter 9

Christ Seen As God's Salvation

Mine eyes have seen thy salvation.
—Luke 2:30

Mine eyes have seen thy salvation." Thousands of times that song of Simeon has been sung by careless, thoughtless people. Surely it is one of those songs that should never come from any but believing lips. To make it merely a part of a liturgy, and for people who ought to be ashamed of their sinful lifestyle to say, *"Mine have seen thy salvation,"* must be an atrocious sin before God. Let everyone who has ventured to use such words as these without having thought of their meaning, confess their sin before God. Let them ask God to make those words true that they have so frivolously uttered. Before they close their eyes in death, may their eyes indeed see God's salvation.

The History of Our Savior

Simeon came into the temple, saw there a little baby, and recognized in that newborn child the promised Savior. As he took that Savior into his arms, he said, *"Mine eyes have seen"*—what? *"Mine eyes have seen thy salvation."* He saw God's salvation—not the worker of the salvation only, but the salvation itself. I gather from this that wherever we see Jesus, we see God's salvation. Wherever our spiritual eyes see the Christ of God, there we see salvation. Whether in Bethlehem's manger or on the cross or on the throne of glory from which He will judge the living and the dead—wherever we see Him, we see the salvation of God.

Let me take your thoughts through the history of our Savior for a moment. Far back into the ages when as yet this world and the sun and moon were not created—when God dwelt alone—in the foreknowledge of God it was apparent that man would sin. He knew that elect men, beloved of Him, would fall in the common ruin. Then came the grand debate, the mighty question to be solved only by the supreme intellect of heaven: "How can sinners be reconciled to God?"

In answer to this question, the covenant was formed, that ancient covenant of which David sang, *"Ordered in all things, and sure"* (2 Sam. 23:5). Jesus, the second person of the blessed Godhead, entered into covenant with His Father. He agreed that in the fullness of time He would stand in the sinner's place and pay the sinner's debt. He would lead as many as the Father gave Him. He would become the Second Adam—the restoring Adam—to them, though through the first and fallen Adam they, with others, had been destroyed. With the signing of this covenant, with the shaking of hands of the divine parties to that great transaction, I see—as I look into that vast eternity and with holy curiosity desire to scan that council chamber—I see God's salvation in the person of Jesus Christ.

156

This was all that could be seen by faith after the world had been created and man had fallen. This was all that could be seen until *"the fulness of the time was come"* (Gal. 4:4). Then Jesus Christ, who had covenanted to save His people, came to perform the work. Oh, the grandeur of that day when angels came in haste to sing that the babe was born in Bethlehem. Ah, Simeon, what you see there is not merely a baby—a little child feeding at his mother's breast—it is the Word incarnate, the Logos without whom *"was not any thing made that was made"* (John 1:3). He who spoke, and it was done, lies there (Ps. 33:9). He who said, *"Let there be light"* (Gen. 1:3), and light was—the Wisdom who was with God when He balanced the clouds and when He established the lights of the universe—even He is there in the person of that child. The son of Mary is also the Son of God. Whenever we study God incarnate, we need to understand the mystery that *"the Word was made flesh, and dwelt among us, (and we* [those chosen by God] *beheld his glory, the glory as of the only begotten of the Father,) full of grace and truth"* (John 1:14). Then, when you see God in human flesh, you see God's salvation.

Follow that baby with the eyes of your love from infancy to adulthood. See Him obeying His earthly father for thirty years, handling the saw and the hammer in the carpenter's shop. *"Being found in fashion as a man, he humbled himself"* (Phil. 2:8). See Him during the three years of His blessed ministry. What work was crowded into those few months! How the zeal of God's house ate Him up (John 2:17)! The dew fell upon Him in the night when He kept the sheep of God in the wilderness and on the side of the mountain, shepherding them with midnight prayers. Oftentimes the sweat fell from Him in that daily service that, as the Servant of Servants, He rendered to all His brothers. No one toiled as He did, so perfectly, so willingly, with so complete a dedication of all His faculties to His all-absorbing work. Behold the righteousness of the saints. This work of Christ is making a robe in which the saints will be arrayed. His active obedience renders to God a payment for our disobedience to His holy law. In Christ, the actively obedient One, you see God's salvation.

But, oh, let your eyes swim with tears as you follow Him from His active to His passive obedience. I just quoted the verse, *"Being found in fashion as a man, he humbled himself"* (Phil. 2:8). As you go on, you read, *"And became obedient unto death, even the death of the cross"* (v. 8). There He is in the Garden of Gethsemane among the olives. Do you hear His sighs, His deep groans? Do you notice the drops of blood as they fall to the earth? He is pleading, *"If it be possible, let this cup pass from me"* (Matt. 26:39), but it is not possible. Do you see Him hurried away with the felon's kiss still upon His cheek—hurried away by traitorous hands to Caiaphas, hurried to Pilate and Herod, one after the other, scorned and scoffed everywhere?

He whose face is as bright as the morning when the sun rises, He it is whom they made nothing of and ridiculed and mocked. Into His face, which angels look on with hushed awe, they cast their accursed spit. They beat Him and said, *"Hail, King of the Jews!"* (Matt. 27:29). They mocked His royalty by crowning Him with thorns. They mocked His priesthood by blindfolding Him and saying, *"Who is he that smote thee?"* (Matt. 26:68). Remember that He who was subjected to this shame is God's salvation. He was made lower than earth's lowest servants, so that He might lift us higher than heaven's brightest angels. He came down from where He was in heaven's excellency to these depths of shame, so that out of all our shame He might lift us up to heavenly excellency.

Then, at length, the torture came to a climax, and the patient sufferer gave His hands to the iron and His feet to the nails. They lifted Him up; He had to die a felon's death. He had to suffer *"without the camp"* (Heb. 13:13). Because He was made sin for us, He could not be in the congregation (Ps. 1:5). He had to be *"numbered with the transgressors"* (Isa. 53:12). Behold Him dying with bodily pains not easily described! But, mind you, the worst was this: God, to whom good men look for help when they die, refused Him help. Jehovah, who had never forsaken the virtuous, forsook Him, the most virtuous of all. He who is our castle and high tower, our rampart and defense in our danger, hid, as it were, His face from Him. Then that bitterest of all cries, which contained in it as much grief as all the shrieks of the damned in hell, went up: *"My God, my God, why hast thou forsaken me?"* (Matt. 27:46). There He was, the forsaken One, yet He was God's salvation, for He was

> Bearing that we might never bear
> His Father's righteous wrath.

He endured being cast away by heaven so that we, low as we are, might be enfolded in the divine bosom and be loved with divine affection.

This is not all. On the third day, He, who had conquered on the cross, rose to claim the victory. Behold Him! He is God's salvation as He rises from the tomb. *"O death, where is thy sting? O* [boastful] *grave, where is thy victory?"* (1 Cor. 15:55). Jehovah-Jesus has saved us from death; He has risen from the sepulcher. Behold Him as He ascends! He rides in solemn splendor up to heaven's gate. Your ears can even now catch the echoes of that song, *"Lift up your heads, O ye gates; and be ye lift up, ye everlasting doors; and the King of glory shall come in"* (Ps. 24:7). He who enters has saved us and has gone to receive gifts for men. His entrance there is the entrance of all His people, for He is their representative, and He takes possession of heaven on their behalf. Since He is there for us, we are saved. His presence on the throne is the presence of God's salvation.

He is still the Lamb that was slain, pleading with His never ceasing, ever prevalent intercession. May your faith anticipate the day when He will come again, not with a sin offering, but unto salvation. When you and I see Him, we will see God's salvation. Our bodies will be perfected, to be weak and to suffer no more. Our bodies will be made like His glorious body. Believers who have gone before us, who at this moment sleep in their silent tombs or in the crowded cemetery or in the cold vault, will also hear the sound of His second coming when the trumpet blast will tell the world that the Lord has come. They will wing their triumphant course

> From beds of dust and silent clay
> To realms of everlasting day.

Jesus Christ will be to them, as He will be to us, God's salvation.

That was Simeon's idea, I think; I have only hammered out his bar of gold a little. "Where Jesus is, there is the salvation of God."

160

My Own Eyes Have Seen His Salvation

Let us look at some pages in our own autobiographies. The text says, *"Mine eyes have seen thy salvation."* Simeon must not be allowed to monopolize these words. I claim them, too. *"Mine eyes have seen thy salvation."* Fellow believer, you can, in a spiritual sense, use the same language as this patriarch Simeon. You, too, can say, *"Mine eyes have seen thy salvation."* Will you look through the book of your life awhile as I look through mine?

Well, we do not need to read those early pages, the pages of our state of sin. Shed tears and blot them out. Dear hand of Jesus, stained with blood, wipe across each one of them and blot them out forever. But what is this first bright page? It is the page that tells how we began to live, the page that records our spiritual birth, and I think we will find written somewhere across it, "This day my eyes beheld God's salvation."

I well remember that day. I had looked here and looked there. This was my question: Since I have offended God, how can He forgive me? It was no use telling me God is merciful; I had an answer for that: "God is just." It was of little avail to say, "Sin is little," for I knew better. It was heavy to me; what must it be to God? The question I wanted answered was, How can God in justice pass by my iniquities?

Then I learned, as in a moment, this sweet story that it has been my delight to tell in various forms a thousand times. Jesus came and said, "I will pay the sinner's debt. I will stand in his place of curse and ruin and will bear for him the penalty of pain. For him I will bear even death." I learned that if I would look—just look and that was all—that if I would simply trust in Jesus, I would be saved. I looked, and, happy day, my eyes saw His salvation! That blessed doctrine of substitution, that simple command, "Believe and live," were the glass through which my soul looked and saw God's salvation.

But if I remember correctly, a little later on—in my case, it was not more than a week after I had been forgiven—I found myself in another difficulty. I found that I could not do what I wanted. My desire was now never to sin again, but I did sin. I willed to be holy, but I was not what I willed to be. I groaned and cried, "How can I be saved from this evil heart of mine, from this corruption of nature?"

I well remember going to the same place where I had heard of the Savior, and I heard the minister declare that if any man found in himself the evil nature, he was not saved. "Ah," I thought, "I know better than that." I could not be persuaded of that. I knew that I was saved. I had looked to Christ. I was where Paul was when he said, *"To will is present with me; but how to perform that which is good I find not"* (Rom. 7:18). I said to myself, "My will is so fickle; how can I hold on? My power is so feeble; how can I stand against sin?"

Ah, and well do I remember the day when I could say in a more emphatic sense than before, *"Mine eyes have seen thy salvation."* For as I searched the Word, I perceived that as many as believed in Christ had eternal life, and eternal life is not a life that lasts only a little while. It is what it is said to be—everlasting life.

Then I perceived in the Word that the old body of sin and death would struggle against this everlasting life. However, it is written that the new life is a living and incorruptible seed *"which liveth and abideth for ever"* (1 Pet. 1:23). And I discovered the apostle's words: *"Thanks be to God, which giveth us the victory through our Lord Jesus Christ"* (1 Cor. 15:57). It was a great discovery when I saw that the life God had given me could not die any more than God could; that it was a gift from Him; that He had made me a partaker *"of the divine nature, having escaped the corruption that is in the world through lust"* (2 Pet. 1:4). I discovered that the Spirit of the Most High was given to the believer to dwell in him and to be with him forever, that He who began the work had declared that He would carry it on and perfect it unto the day of the appearing of our Lord and Savior, Jesus Christ (Phil. 1:6).

When I learned that truth, I felt as if I had not seen God's salvation before. I had seen so little of it the first time, but enough to make me leap for joy, it is true! But on the second discovery, I beheld that He who redeemed me from the guilt of sin would quite as certainly redeem me from the power of sin. I found that He who set me on the rock would keep me there, that He who put me on the road had said about all His servants, *"I will put my fear in their hearts, that they shall not depart from me"* (Jer. 32:40). That was a glorious discovery! I did not have one of the vacillating salvations that some people profess to have, that only last for a day or two, or a few weeks at the most, and then depart—in Christ today and out of Christ tomorrow. Christ has pardoned their sin, yet they think He has not given them salvation! But to know that *"the gifts and calling of God are without repentance"* (Rom. 11:29), this is to see God's salvation in a broader light.

He has given us His precious promises: *"He that believeth and is baptized shall be saved"* (Mark 16:16). *"The righteous also shall hold on his way, and he that hath clean hands shall be stronger and*

163

stronger" (Job 17:9). The Word of Christ stands sure: *"I give unto* [my sheep] *eternal life; and they shall never perish, neither shall any man pluck them out of my hand"* (John 10:28). I pray that every reader who has seen Christ may go on to see more of Christ until he has seen his full security in the person of the Well Beloved.

A long time after I had made these discoveries, I once again found afresh that Christ is God's salvation. I discovered partly through thought, and partly through the clear testimony of the written Word, that every soul who believes in Christ does so because God made him believe in Christ. Concerning that soul, God purposed that he would be a believer. That purpose was made from all eternity—was made before the earth ever existed—and that purpose, once made, could never be changed. It was like the mountains of brass that could never be moved. The salvation of the believer in Christ did not rest on his own will, but on God's will. The purpose that saved him was not his own purpose, even as it is written, *"It is not of him that willeth, nor of him that runneth, but of God that showeth mercy"* (Rom. 9:16).

Why, I remember that that discovery about salvation was as wonderful to me as was the very first. It was almost like another conversion! I had been up to my ankles in the water of life before, but now I was up to my chest, and I could say nothing but this:

I'm a monument of grace,
　　A sinner saved by blood,
The streams of love I trace
　　Up to the fount of God;
And in His sacred bosom see
　　Eternal thoughts of love to me.

Here it was that my eyes saw God's salvation—saw the source of it, the secret springs of it, the eternity of it, the immutability of it, and the divinity of it. I pray that every burdened child of God may get to see that also. Then he will sing for joy.

Probably, dear believer, we have not all gone further than that, or even that far. But it is a very blessed thing when we are led to see another truth, namely, that every believer is one with Jesus Christ. We are members of His body, of His flesh and of His bones. The Christ in heaven is the same Christ who is here on earth in every one of His saved ones; they are all parts of Him. There is a vital union existing between them, so that they are whatever Christ is. They were one with Him in eternity, and they were one in the grave, one when He rose, one when He triumphed over His foes. They are one with Him as

> Now in heaven He takes His seat,
> And angels sing all hell's defeat.

Every believer is as much one with Christ as the finger is one with the body. If I lost my finger, I would not be a perfect man, as far as my body is concerned. And if Christ lost the lowliest member of His body, it would be a part of Christ that would be lost, and Christ would not be a perfect Christ. We are one with Jesus by indissoluble, vital union, and if your soul perceives this, you will clap your hands and say to the Father, "I have seen Your salvation indeed, for now I see that I am in heaven." He *"hath raised us up together, and made us sit together in heavenly places in Christ Jesus"* (Eph. 2:6). We are saved and glorified in Christ Jesus, who is our Representative and covenant Head.

I have not exhausted this theme yet, and I only pray that you and I may go on to know more and more the heights and depths of God's salvation. If we would ever be permitted to look down from heaven upon the world of misery, if in some future state we would gaze into that land of darkness and despair where sinners who are cast away from God are suffering the due punishment for their sins, if our eyes would ever see their agonies and our ears ever hear their cries of despair, we would, among other things, say, "Dear Father, I never knew before how great Your salvation is, for I also would be there except for Your mercy. Until I saw what hell is like, I did not know how much I owed You. I could not say that my eyes had seen Your salvation in its heights and depths."

Let us put a better, more pleasing light on the subject. Let us talk about the time

> When I stand before the throne
> Dressed in beauty not my own.

I will see Him, for it is written, *"Whom I shall see for myself, and mine eyes shall behold, and not another"* (Job 19:27). You and I will cast our crowns at His feet. We will raise our voices with all the white-robed throng in everlasting hallelujahs. Then we will say, "My Father, *'mine eyes have seen thy salvation.'"*

Your Eyes Can See His Salvation

Some who are reading this have never seen God's salvation. The Gospel is hidden to them, and if it is hidden, it is not hidden because I have used confusing words to hide it. *"If our gospel be hid, it is hid to them that are lost: in whom the god of this world hath blinded the minds of them which believe not"* (2 Cor. 4:3-4). Blind sinner, do you desire to see the

166

salvation of God? Ah, do you say, "If I know my own heart, I do"? Why can you not see it, then? His salvation is very plain. Oh, I understand—your eyes are blinded. They are covered by scales.

The first scale I see over your eyes—and, oh, I wish I could take it off for you—is this: You do not even believe that you need any salvation. The man who does not believe he needs saving will, of course, never see God's salvation. In your heart you say, *"I am rich, and increased with goods, and have need of nothing"* (Rev. 3:17). My poor friend, be persuaded to accept God's opinion of you, which is much nearer the truth than yours. *"Thou art wretched, and miserable, and poor, and blind, and naked"* (v. 17). You are lost, ruined, and condemned, as it is written, *"He that believeth not is condemned already"* (John 3:18). Do you see what I am saying? Has that scale dropped from your eyes?

Now I see another scale (I wish that I could take that off, too), and that is, you do not know that you are blind. You say, "I must try to save myself." This is a very thick scale. You will never see while that is on your eyes. Do you not notice how Simeon put it? He did not say, "My eyes have seen my own salvation"; he said, *"Mine eyes have seen thy salvation,"* referring to God's salvation, the Lord's salvation. Let me tell you, poor sinner, if you are ever going to be saved, salvation must be God's in the beginning, God's in the middle, and God's in the end. No salvation will ever save your soul except one that is divine from top to bottom.

If nature's fingers could nimbly spin a garment that would cover human nakedness, it would be of no use. All that nature spins, God must unravel before a soul can be clothed in the righteousness of Christ. It is not your works; it is Christ's works that

167

must save you. It is not your tears, but Christ's blood. It is not your feelings, not anything in you or from you. Listen, for you have an ear to hear: *"Salvation is of the LORD"* (Jonah 2:9), of the Lord from first to last. Oh, if that scale comes off your eyes, I know that you will say, "Now that I begin to see, I see enough to know that I cannot see. I have just enough light to discover the darkness I am in. I see that none can save me but God. He must do it. But will He do it? Will He save me?"

Lend me your finger, blind sinner. Do you see the hem of Jesus' garment? Of course you do not, but touch that with your finger, and your sight will be restored at once. I mean this. Jesus died to save sinners such as you. Trust Him, and you are saved; you are saved completely and at once.

A physician who had some concern about his soul asked a godly patient of his, "Can you explain to me what faith is?" "Yes," said his godly patient, "I can show it to you now if God will let you see it. It is like this. You see, I am very ill. I cannot help myself, and I do not attempt to help myself, but I have confidence in you. I put myself into your care. I take the medicine you give me, and I do what you tell me. That is faith. You must entrust yourself to the hands of Christ like that." That is it. When you, my dear friend, wholly and entirely entrust yourself to the hands of Christ, then your eyes have seen God's salvation.

I want to say one more thing to everyone who has seen God's salvation. Perhaps you are poor. Well, if that is the case, say to yourself, "I am poor, but *'mine eyes have seen thy salvation.'*" Perhaps you are suffering. Then say, "I feel sick, but never mind. *'Mine eyes have seen thy salvation.'*" Perhaps you have had some warnings and hints that you will soon

168

be called to die. Never mind; do not fret. Your eyes have seen God's salvation. How much better to die in an attic or in a ditch and see God's salvation, than to be carried in the most pompous ceremony to your grave as one who knows nothing of God and of the Savior.

Oh, you who are much tried and much troubled, bear up, bear up; your sorrow will not last much longer. When you and I get to heaven, as I trust we will, as I know we will if we are resting on the atonement of Christ, these troubles along the way will only be cause for us to say to one another, "How graciously the Lord has held us in His providence, and how wonderfully He has brought us through every trial! Even in my poverty, my eyes saw His salvation. In my sickness and in my death, I only saw it all the more clearly because of the clouds and darkness that were around me!"

God bless you, dear reader. May you indeed see God's salvation.

Chapter 10

The Hope That Purifies

*Beloved, now are we the sons of God, and it doth not
yet appear what we shall be: but we know that, when
he shall appear, we shall be like him; for we shall see
him as he is. And every man that hath this hope in
him purifieth himself, even as he is pure.*
—*1 John 3:2–3*

The Christian is a person of many present joys.
"Beloved, now are we the sons of God," and,
being God's sons, we cannot be altogether
unhappy. Relationship to the ever blessed God must
bring with it a measure of joy. *"Happy art thou, O
Israel,"* sang Moses. *"Who is like unto thee, O people
saved by the LORD?"* (Deut. 33:29). Those who can
truly be called the sons of God are a blessed people.

Nonetheless, the main portion of the believer's
inheritance lies in the future. It is not so much
what I have as what I will have that makes me joyful. *"It doth not yet appear what we shall be."* To
the unbeliever, all that is to come is darkness. He
can expect to go from the dimness of evening to the
blackness of a midnight that will never end. But for
the Christian, *"light is sown"* (Ps. 97:11). The
Christian is in darkness now—the only darkness he

will ever know—and from the twilight of the morning he will enter into the perfect day—a day whose sun will never set. We have the eyes of hope given to us. Looking confidently at the narrow stream of death and looking beyond to that place that carnal eyes cannot see, we, with these farseeing eyes, behold the glory that is to be revealed, and we are blessed with the joys of hope. Let every Christian, therefore, whenever he is discouraged about things of the present, refresh his soul with thoughts of the future.

We have often spoken of the past, and I know that we have frequently been comforted by seeing how graciously God has dealt with us in bringing us up out of the pit. Now, we will get further consolation by seeing what is to become of us in the future yet to be revealed. However, my objective at this time will not be to impart consolation as much as to excite to holiness. Our text is a practical one, and while it deals with hope, it has more to do with the result of that hope, which is purity in the believer's life.

The Believer's Hope

To begin, then, let us look at the believer's hope. The text speaks of people who have hope—*"hope in him"*—which I understand to mean hope in Jesus Christ.

To Be Like Jesus

The Christian has a hope that only Christians have. It is the hope of being like Jesus Christ. *"We shall be like him; for we shall see him as he is."* Now, some would not put it quite that way; they would say that their hope as Christians is to tread the golden streets, pass through the pearly gates, listen to the musicians with their harps, and, standing on the sea of glass, be forever free from toil and pain. But those are only the lower joys of heaven, except as far as they indicate spiritual bliss. I do believe that there are some who profess to be Christians who would like Muhammad's heaven and would be perfectly satisfied if they could sit on a green and flowery hill and could drink from rivers of milk and honey.

However, after all, the real truth, the truth that is contained in these metaphors and figures of speech and that underlies them all, is that the heaven a true Christian seeks is a spiritual one. It is the heaven of being like the Lord. While heaven will consist of our sharing in the Redeemer's power, the Redeemer's joy, and the Redeemer's honor, it appears from the text that it consists mainly of our sharing the Redeemer's purity. The joy of heaven lies mainly in our being spiritually and morally like Him, being purified as He is pure. I must frankly confess that, of all my expectations of heaven, I would cheerfully renounce ten thousand things if I could only feel that I will have perfect holiness. For if I can become like Jesus Christ and share His character—pure and perfect—I do not understand how any other joy can be denied me. If we will have that, surely we will have everything. This, then, is our hope—that we will be like Him, for we will see Him as He is.

In a moral sense, every man sees what he himself is. A man who is bad sees evil; he is blind to good. The man who is partially like Christ has only a partial view of Christ. You can almost know your own character by your view of Jesus. If your eye does not see inexpressible beauty in Him, it is your eye that is to blame, for *"he is altogether lovely"* (Song 5:16). When the eye of our inward nature comes to see Jesus as He is, then we may be sure that we are like Him. It is the pure in heart who see God (Matt. 5:8), because God, the inexpressibly pure One, can only be seen by those who are themselves pure.

When we are perfectly pure, we will be able to understand Christ. When we understand Christ, when we *"see him as he is,"* as we will at His appearing, then we will be like Him. Like Him, we will be free from sin. Like Him, we will be full of consecration to God. Like Him, we will be pure and perfect. Today He is Conqueror over sin and death and hell; He is supreme in His virtue and His holiness; He has conquered all the powers of evil. And one day we, too, will put our foot on the Dragon's head. We, too, will see sin bruised beneath us and will emerge more than conquerors through Him who has loved us (Rom. 8:37). This, then, is our hope, that we will be like our Head when we see Him.

The Grounds of Our Hope

Why do we expect this? What are the grounds of our hope? The context shows us that we cannot expect to be like Christ because of anything that is in us by nature or by any efforts that we ourselves can make. The basis of everything is divine love. Observe that the chapter of our text begins, *"Behold, what manner of love the Father hath bestowed upon us, that we should be called the sons of God"* (1 John 3:1). We expect to be like Christ, the beloved of God, because we are also beloved of God. It is the nature of the love of God to make its object like God. Therefore, we expect that love will work with light and purity and make us into light and purity, too.

The third chapter of 1 John goes on to say that we have been called sons of God and really are His children. Well, that is another ground of our hope: we hope to be like Christ because the sons of God are like each other. The Lord has said that Jesus Christ will be the firstborn among many brothers. Whom God loved *"he also did predestinate to be conformed to the image of his Son, that he might be the firstborn among many brethren"* (Rom. 8:29). Very well, then. Since we are adopted into the divine family and are to be made like the Elder Brother, we, therefore, believe that we will one day be like the Lord Jesus Christ in the perfection of His excellence.

Then we have this further support for our hope, if it is not a main pillar of it, that we are now one with Jesus Christ. Therefore, *"when he shall appear, we shall be like him"* (1 John 3:2). There is an intimate connection between our spirits and Christ. He is hidden; therefore, we are hidden, and the world does not know us. He is to be revealed—there is to be a day of His manifestation to angels and to men—and when He is manifested, we will be manifested, too. Knowing that we are united to Christ by sacred, mysterious bonds, we therefore expect that when we see Him as He is, we will be like Him.

Still, for simplicity's sake, it is good to say that the basis of our hope lies altogether in Him. *"Every man that hath this hope in him* [Christ] *purifieth himself."* Beloved, all true hope is hope in Christ. If your hope lies in yourself, it is a delusion. If your hope lies in any earthly priest and not in this one High Priest of our faith, your hope is a lie. If your hope stands with one foot on the work of Christ and the other foot on your own resolutions or merits, your hope will fail you. Hope in Him is the only hope that can be acceptable to God, the only hope that will bear the stress of your weight, the only hope that will stand the test of the hour of trial and the Day of Judgment.

Our hope, then, of being like Christ is a hope in Christ. We are trusting Him; we are depending on Him. If He does not make us like Himself, our hope is gone. If we are ever to get to heaven, it will be through Him and through Him alone. Our hope is in Him from top to bottom. He is our Alpha and Omega—the beginning and end. There our hope begins, and there our hope ends. You, O Christ, are all our confidence! We know of none besides. This, then, is the believer's hope—a hope to be made like Christ; a hope based on Christ.

The Operation of Hope on the Soul

Now, in a more practical light, our text speaks of the operation that hope has on the soul. *"Every man that hath this hope in him purifieth himself."*

Hope Does Not Cause Pride

Hope does not puff a person up; it purifies. I know there are some who say, "Well, if I had a hope, a sure hope—full assurance that I would go to heaven—I think I would feel that I am somebody." Yes, very likely you would, but then you do not possess such a hope, and God does not mean to give it to you while you are in your present condition. But when the Lord makes a person His child, He takes away his evil heart. When He shows a person His great love for him, He humbles him; He lays him low. Therefore, the expectation of heaven and of perfection never exalts a man.

If any man can say, "I am sure of heaven and proud of it," he can take my word for it that he is sure of hell! If your religion puffs you up, get rid of your religion, for it is not worth anything. He who grows great in his own estimation through the love of God does not know the love of God, for the love of God is like the fish that the Lord put into Peter's boat: the fuller the boat was, the more it began to sink. O Lord, the more the glories of Your love strike my eyes, the humbler I will be.

Hope Does Not Give License to Sin

Again, a person who has this hope of heaven—actually, according to our text, this hope of perfection—finds that it does not give license to sin. I have heard some say, "If I had a good hope and knew I would go to heaven, I would live as I liked." Perhaps you would, but you do not have this hope, and God will not give it to you while you are in such a state that you would like to live in sin.

If a Christian could live as he liked, how would he live? Why, he would live without sin. If the Lord were to indulge the newborn nature of His own children with unrestricted liberty, in that unrestricted liberty they would run after holiness. The unrenewed heart would like to sin, but the renewed heart quite as eagerly loves to obey the Lord. When the Lord has changed you, He can give you not only a hope, but a full assurance that that hope will come true. Yet, you will walk all the more carefully with your God, for he *that hath this hope in him purifieth himself, even as he is pure.*

Hope Leads to Holiness

This hope, then, does not puff up and does not lead to a license to sin. You can see why it is so.

176

Gratitude leads to holiness. Anyone who can say, "God has saved me, and I am on my way to being made like Christ," will also say, "I owe all this to God; how can I show Him my gratitude?" He must be a brute, he must be a devil, he must be seven thousand devils in one, if he says, "God is doing all this for me; therefore, I will continue in sin." The apostle Paul did well to say of such people that their damnation is just (Rom. 3:8). But where there is the good hope of heaven, the person naturally says, "O my Lord, have You loved me so well, and have You provided such a glorious portion for me hereafter? Now I will obey You; I will serve You. Help me to run in the ways of Your commandments (Ps. 119:32)."

Such a person, when led by the Spirit, also feels that holiness is in line with his expectations. He expects to be like Christ. "Very well, then," he says. "I will try to be like Christ. If I am to possess a perfect nature one day, the most natural thing is that I should begin to seek after it now." If the Lord intends to make you an heir of immortality to dwell at His right hand, does it seem right that you should go and live as others do? Suppose you know right now that before long you will be at God's right hand. Does it not seem a shameful thing that you should go and become a drunkard, or that you should be dishonest? *It is not for kings to drink wine; nor for princes strong drink*" (Prov. 31:4), and, surely, it is not for children of God to drink the wines of sin and to go after the sweets of iniquity. It is not for princes of the imperial blood, descended from the King of Kings, to play with the filthy lewdness of this age and with the sins of earth.

Surely an angel would not stoop to be a crow. In the same way, it is not congruous, it is not fitting, that he who is a brother to Christ and is to dwell forever where Jesus is, should be found in the haunts of sin. It is very natural and fitting that the child of God, who has the blessing of God's Spirit, should purify himself, since he expects to be completely like Christ before long.

The Believer Purifies Himself

Now, let us take a closer look at what it means for the believer to purify himself. If we are very orthodox, we can afford to use language that does not look orthodox, but people who are unorthodox usually have to be extremely guarded in what they say. Now, I do not actually believe that any man purifies himself, yet the text says that *"every man that hath this hope in him* [Christ] *purifieth himself."* We believe that the Holy Spirit purifies people. We trust in Christ's blood to purify us.

> Let the water and the blood
> From the riven side that flowed
> Be of sin the double cure.

We lay all purity at God's feet, believing that He is the Creator of it. Still, the text says that *"every man that hath this hope in him purifieth himself."* There must be a meaning in this, and the fact that God purifies us must also be true while this is true. Here is the meaning of the text: God the Holy Spirit works in every person who has a true hope, so that he diligently strives to become purified and uses all means to overcome sin and to walk in righteousness. While you read about this truth in this chapter, may you examine yourself. When a person has a true hope in Christ, he begins to purify himself by the power of the Holy Spirit.

From Grosser Sins

First, he puts away all the grosser sins. Perhaps, before conversion, he had been immoral. He had been lewd in language and in act. He had been dishonest. He had been a blasphemer. Conversion does away with all that. I have been astonished and delighted when I have seen how readily these sins are put to death. They are taken out and executed. Many who never lived a day without swearing have never had a temptation to swear from the moment of their conversion. God will change the heart so thoroughly that these grosser sins go at once.

But there are sins of the flesh that, though we are purged from them, will endeavor to return. Therefore, the person who has a hope of heaven will purify himself every day from them. He will hate the very thought of those sins and any expressions or actions that might tend toward them. He abhors them; he flees from them. He knows that if he begins to toy with them, he will soon go from bad to worse. He understands that in this warfare, to flee is the truest courage; therefore, from such sins of the flesh he daily flees as Joseph did, even if he has to leave his garment behind him, so that he can get away from them. He purifies himself.

From Evil Company

Then he purifies himself from all evil company. Those people whom he once thought the best of friends he now avoids. If they will go with him to heaven, he will be glad to have them join his company, but if they will neither repent of sin nor believe in Jesus, he says to them, "You can be of no further service to me." If he can help them to heaven, he seeks them out and tries to win them. But, when they ridicule him, he is afraid that their example might be injurious to him, and he keeps away from them and seeks better company. He purifies himself.

From Day One

The believer seeks to purify himself from the day of his conversion to the day that he dies. Perhaps, at first, he does not know some things to be sin that he afterward finds out to be so. As the light gradually shines into his soul, he puts away this and that and the other sin with a strong and resolute hand. If there was some sin that pleased him much, that was to him like a right hand or a right eye, he cuts it off or tears it out (Matt. 5:29–30). For, having a hope of heaven in him, he knows he cannot take any sin to heaven, and he does not want to. He puts it away. He knows he must put it away before he can enter into eternal life.

Soon he finds out that there are certain sins in his nature that more readily overcome him than others. Against these he sets a double watch. Possibly he has a quick temper. Over this he grieves very much, and he prays to God twice as much, "Lord, conquer my temper! Keep my tongue, lest I say bitter words. Keep my heart, lest I indulge in unkind feelings." If the job in which he finds himself involves sin (and most professions have some particular sin), he says, "Then I will have nothing to do with it. If I cannot make money without sin, I will lose money or change my business, but I will not sin."

He observes some sin that runs in his family; he knows that his household has some particular fault. Here, again, he cries to God, "Lord, purify me and purify my house from this!" He observes that there are certain sins in the city where he lives. Against these he cries. He knows that there are sins characteristic of his position in life. Is he a rich man? He is afraid of growing worldly. Is he a poor man? He is afraid of becoming envious. He looks at his position and observes what the particular sins of that position are. Then, in the power of the eternal Spirit, he seeks to purify himself from each one of these sins.

Perhaps he is traveling for his health. He knows that many travelers, though they profess to be Christians, never observe the Sabbath; they forget, to a large extent, the regular habits of devotion that they had at home. So he sets a double watch over himself in that respect. Is he in great trial? Then he knows that temptations to be impatient and to murmur will come, and he tries to purify himself from these. Is he enjoying great pleasure? Then he knows the temptation will be to make this world his home, and so he tries to purify himself from that.

You see, beloved, under the power of God's Spirit, this purifying of the life is a great work to be done, but it is a work that every person who has this hope in Christ will do. If he is indeed hoping in the Lord Jesus, it will be the great struggle and warfare of his life to get rid of this sin and then another sin, so that he may be sanctified unto the Lord—a holy man, prepared for a holy heaven.

How Does the Believer Purify Himself?

Now, then, how does the believer purify himself? I have shown what he does, but by what means does he do it?

By Noting the Example of Christ

He does it, first, by noting the example of Christ. The hoping man reads about Christ's life and says, "Here is my model, but I fall far short of it. O God, give me all that there is in Christ! Take off from my character all the imperfections, for they must be imperfections if they are not in Christ." By familiarizing himself with the life of his Savior and by communing with Christ, he is helped to see where sin is and to hate it.

By Praying for a Tender Conscience

He asks God to give him a tender conscience. Oh, I wish more Christians had a tender conscience. I have heard of blind people who try to learn to read with their fingers late in life. Unfortunately, some have had manual labors to perform that have hardened their fingers, preventing them from reading. I am afraid that some Christians have hard consciences—two or three thicknesses of skin over them. They need to have the surgical knife used to make their consciences tender again.

It is a blessed thing to have a conscience that will shiver when the very ghost of a sin goes by. We do not want a conscience that is like our great steamships at sea; they do not yield to every wave. We want a conscience that is like a cork on the water; it goes up and down with every ripple. We want to be instantly sensitive to the very approach of sin. May God make us so. This sensitivity the Christian endeavors to have, for he knows that if he does not have it, he will never be purified from his sin.

By Keeping His Eyes on God

The hopeful believer always tries to keep his eyes on God and not on men. That is an important aspect of purity. I know many people whose main thought is of other people's opinions. They ask, "What will people say? What will the neighbors say? What will be the common opinion about it?" You will never be holy until you do not care the least bit about what anybody says except your God. A thing that is right is right anywhere. If it is right before the Lord, it is right even if the world should boo it.

Oh, that we had more moral courage, for moral courage is essential to true holiness. The man who has this hope in him will not say, "If the door is shut and nobody hears about it, I may feel free to do the evil," or, "I am in a different country where the customs differ; therefore, I will do as others do." No, such hypocrisy shows a rotten heart. The man of God will say, "This is right before the Lord, and, though no one sees me to commend me, though every tongue should speak against me to blame me, it is the same to me. I will do right and shun evil." Keeping his eyes on God is one way by which the Christian purifies himself.

By Learning from Other People's Lives

The hopeful believer notes the lives of others and makes them his beacons. If you were steering down the river in a vessel and saw a boat ahead of you run into a sandbar, you would not go there to find out where the true channel was. You would let other shipwrecks be your beacons. Even so, the Christian, when he observes a fault in another, does not stand there and say, "Ah, see how faulty that man is!" No, he says, "Let me shun that fault." And when he sees the virtue of another, if his heart is right, he does not begin to pick holes in it and say,

"He is not as good as he looks," but he says, "Lord, there is a sweet flower in that man's garden! Give me some of the seed of it. Let it grow in my soul." So other men become both his beacon and his example.

Through a Heart-Searching Ministry

A wise Christian tries to purify himself by involving himself in a heart-searching ministry. If a ministry never cuts you, it is of no use to you. If it does not make you feel ashamed of yourself—yes, and sometimes half angry with the preacher—it is not good for much. If it is all rubbing the fur the right way and making you feel happy and comfortable, be afraid of it, be afraid of it. But if, on the contrary, it opens up old wounds and makes the sores fester and makes the soul bleed before the living God, you can hope that it is the hand of one whom God is using for your lasting good. The true Christian not only wishes the preacher to search him, but he prays to God, *"Search me, O God, and know my heart: try me, and know my thoughts"* (Ps. 139:23). He does not want to live in a sin, thinking that it is not a sin, but he wants to get away from it.

I am afraid that some Christians do not want to know too much about Christ's commands because there might be some very awkward ones that they do not want to obey. They are very pleased if they can get somebody to say that some of Christ's commandments are nonessential and unimportant. Ah, dear friend, whoever dares to say that anything that Christ says is unimportant is a traitor to his Master. It is always important for a servant to do as his Master tells him, and it is essential to our comfort and obedience that whatever the Lord has spoken we should try to perform in His strength.

184

The hopeful Christian endeavors to purify himself by setting before himself Christ as his standard. He purifies himself, even as Christ is pure. My dear friend, we will make a mistake if we rely completely on any man to be our model except the Lord Jesus Christ, for in anybody's life there will be sure to be something in excess. I am certain that it will be best for us, if we are Wesleyans, not to always try to do everything as John Wesley would do it. If we are Calvinists, as much as we should honor John Calvin, we must remember that we will go wrong if we try to season everything with the spirit of John Calvin. No man is fit to be a model for all men except the Savior who redeemed men.

In white all the colors are blended. A perfectly white substance combines all the colors of the rainbow, which are merged in true proportion, while green or indigo or red are only the reflections of a part of the solar rays. In the same way, John, Peter, Paul—these are parts of the light of heaven. These are different colors, and there is beauty in each one of them. But, if you want to get the whole, you must go to Christ, the perfect Lord, for all the light is in Him. In Him is not the red or the blue, but in Him is light, the true light, the whole of it. You are sure to get a lopsided character if you copy any man. However, if we copy Christ, we will attain perfect maturity through the power of His Spirit.

By Perseverance

Oh, believer, what a lifelong task is here for you! He *"that hath this hope in him purifieth himself, even as he is pure."* We will never be able, beloved, to throw down the tools and say, "Now I am finished. I have no more sin to fight against, no more evil to overcome." I have heard of some believers who say that, but I think it must be a mistake. If there is a possibility of getting to that condition, I intend to get to it, and I would urge you to go after it. But I think that until you die you will have some evil to struggle with. As long as you are in this body, there will be enough kindling for one of the Devil's sparks to try to light. You will need to keep throwing water on it, and every moment be on the watchtower, even until you cross the Jordan.

Fighting sin is our lifelong business, and, beloved, I do not know that you can have a better business. For while you are contending against sin, purifying yourself by the precious blood, you will be bringing honor to God. Your heart will become a field in which the power and grace of God will be displayed, for He will come and purify you. He will be the real Purifier while He is using you to purify yourself.

Our Text Is a Test

We can use this precious text as a test. *"Every man that hath this hope in him purifieth himself."* Dear reader, the question is, Do we have a true hope in Christ? If we do, we purify ourselves; we strive to purify ourselves as Christ is pure.

Now, there are some professing Christians who go to the opposite of this: they defile themselves. Yes, they defile themselves. It is a shame that I should have to say it. They were baptized after professing their faith, but they were never cleansed from their old sins. I have heard of people going to the Communion table who also go to the taverns to get drunk. He who has the true hope in Him purifies himself. How can you be said to have that hope if you love such sin? I have heard of professing Christians—and I have been embarrassed to hear of it—who are immoral, who sing immoral songs and do immoral acts, and yet say that they have a hope of heaven. Oh, immoral person, do not deceive yourself. You lie! If you are not pure and chaste, you are not God's child. You may fall into sin by surprise, but if you calmly and deliberately go to that which is unclean, how can you say that the love of God dwells in you?

I knew a man who liked to hear a good sermon and also liked to mingle with those who frequent the tavern and sing immoral songs. He participated in the deeds of his wicked companions. Well, do not be mistaken. *"He that committeth sin is of the devil"* (1 John 3:8). There is no making any excuses and apologies. If you are a lover of sin, you will go where sinners go. If you who live after this fashion say that you have believed in the precious blood of Christ, I do not believe you. If you had a true faith in that precious blood, you would hate sin. If you dare to say that you are trusting in the Atonement while you live in sin, you lie. You are not trusting in the Atonement, for where there is a real faith in the atoning sacrifice, it purifies the man and makes him hate the sin that shed the Redeemer's blood.

After all, holiness is the test. So let the great fan throw the chaff and the wheat together, and let the wind go through and blow the chaff away. You may go to church and sit as God's people sit and sing as God's people sing, but, ah, you may be a disgrace to the profession you make. May God forgive you. May He give you grace to repent of your sin and come to Jesus Christ and find pardon in His precious blood! This is, after all, the test: *"Every man that hath this hope in him purifieth himself."* How can a person have that hope in Christ if he defiles himself?

But there are some others who, while they do not actually defile themselves, let things go very much as a matter of course. They certainly do not purify themselves; they go with the current. If there is a good tone at home, they do not object to it. If there is an evil tone, they do not rebuke it. If they are in the shop and someone speaks about religion, they chime in. If anybody ridicules it, perhaps they do not join in, but they are very quiet and slip away to a corner. They never take sides with Christ, except when everybody else is on His side. True, they do not take sides with the Devil, but they intend to be neutral and uncommitted.

Well, if this describes you, you will slip, one of these days, into your appointed place, and that, I think, ought to be a particularly low place in hell. A sinner who is an out-and-out sinner is a respectable sort of a person, but those low creatures who try to get enough religion to cheat the Devil, but never come straight out and avow Christ—why, I think they deserve a double perdition. They know better. They prove their knowledge by a little sneaking affection for what is right, yet they cleave to evil. The dead fish that floats down the stream has only one fault, but down the stream it goes for that one fault. The man who gives himself up to the current in which he is, proves himself to be spiritually dead.

What, sir! Do you never say no? Do you never put your foot down and say, "I will not do this"? Others have to fight to win the crown, and you expect to get it by lying in bed. Do you think there are crowns in heaven for those who never fight their sins? Do you believe there are rewards in heaven for those who never followed Christ and never endured hardship for His sake? No, make no mistake; you do not know what the truth is.

The truth is in that famous illustration in *The Pilgrim's Progress* by John Bunyan. While I tell it, may you be moved to make that analogy true. As the story goes, the pilgrim saw that the Interpreter's house was a beautiful palace, and on top of it there walked many people clothed in gold. From the roof there came the sweetest music that mortal ear had ever heard. He felt that he would like to be on top of that palace with those who were so happily basking in the sun. So he went to find the way there, but he saw a number of armed men at the door who pushed back every person who sought to enter.

The pilgrim stood back in amazement. But he noticed at a nearby table someone with a pen and an inkwell. A brave man from the crowd, with a determined look, came up and said, "Write my name down, sir!" When his name was written down on the roll, he at once drew his sword and began to fight the armed men. The fight was long and cruel, and he was wounded, but he did not give up the conflict until he had cut his way through, making a living lane through those who had opposed him. So he pressed his way in, and the singers on top of the palace welcomed him with sweet music, singing,

> Come in, come in!
> Eternal glory thou shalt win.

Now, if you want to go to heaven, it is all by grace and through the precious blood of Christ. It is all by simple faith in Christ. Yet, every man who gets there must fight for it. There is no crown except for warriors; there are rewards for none except those who contend for the mastery against flesh and blood, against Satan and against sin.

Whose name will be written down next? Is there a person with a determined look whom God has made resolute against sin? God will write his name down. Only, when your name is written down, remember that he who puts on his armor must not boast as though he takes it off (1 Kings 20:11). There is much that you will never perform unless the eternal God is behind you. Nonetheless, if you have this hope in you, if you have received this hope from God, if it is a hope based on sonship, on divine love—a *"hope in him,"* even in Christ—you will win the day. You will purify yourself, *"even as he is pure."* And, when He appears, you will be like Him, for you will see Him as He is.

I ask the Lord to bless this chapter to every reader. He will have the glory.

Chapter 11

Increasing Your Faith

How is it that ye have no faith?
—Mark 4:40

This question may be very properly asked of those who have no faith at all, and I intend to pose it to them in the second part of this chapter. But it was originally asked of men who had some faith, men who had enough faith to make them disciples of Christ, faith that brought them to sail in the same ship with Him. Even when they reproached Him and said, *"Master, carest thou not that we perish?"* (Mark 4:38), they had faith enough to call Him *"Master."* Yet, in comparison with the faith that they should have had, Christ called their faith no faith at all. They were so wavering, so tossed about with unbelief, that though they were His hearty, honest, and sincere followers, He spoke to them as if they were unbelievers. He asked them, *"How is it that ye have no faith?"*

Those Who Are Christians

First, let me speak to God's people about this painful and puzzling question.

191

Let me say, to begin with, that this question must have been very painful to the One who asked it. The faith in which the disciples were lacking was faith in Him—their Master, their Lord who had loved them before the foundation of the world and who intended to shed His precious blood for them to make them His companions in glory. Yet, they had no faith in Him! Let the Lord Jesus come to you, beloved, and I think you will detect much sorrow in the tone of His voice when He says, "*How is it that ye have no faith,*' or so little faith in Me? I have loved you; to the death I have loved you. Remember Gethsemane and Golgotha. Remember all that I did, and am still doing, for you. How is it that you doubt Me?" Beloved, if we doubt our fellowmen, it is not strange, for Judas is one of a large family. But to doubt the Savior, the faithful and true Friend who sticks closer than a brother (Prov. 18:24), this is a cut as unkind as any of the lashes that fell upon His shoulders when He was chastised in Pilate's hall.

You will see that the question pained Him if you notice to whom He addressed it. "*How is it that ye have no faith?*' You are the chosen Twelve. You have been with Me from the beginning. To you I have expounded the mysteries that have remained dark sayings to the multitude. How is it that My choicest friends, the chosen ones of My group, have no faith in Me?"

And the Lord seems to say to some of us, "*How is it that ye have no faith?*' You are written in My book. No, you are written on My hands and engraved on My heart. You have been bought with My blood, snatched out of the jaws of the lion by My precious power, and restored from all your wanderings by My loving care. How is it that you—My favorites, the King's own chosen companions—how is it that you have no faith?"

And the question was painful for yet another reason, namely, that they had no faith concerning a matter in which one would have thought they would have believed. They were in the ship with Him, and if the ship were to go to the bottom, they would go to the bottom in good company. Yet, they did not have enough faith in Him to believe that He would save their lives. Perhaps they knew His ability; if so, they questioned His willingness. Perhaps they knew His willingness; if so, they questioned His ability. In either case, it was very painful that they would think their own dear Friend, their Lord and Master, would let them sink when the glance of His eye could save them or the will of His heart could deliver them.

And now, this question, as Jesus Christ puts it to us, must be very painful to Him. "Do you not, My children, do you not believe Me? Mine is an unchangeable love, a love that is stronger than death, a love that led Me down into the grave for you. Do you not believe Me? If others doubt Me, I can endure their unbelief, but unbelief from you, My acquaintances, My own familiar friends—oh, this is hard! You have sat under My shadow, and do you doubt Me? You have eaten My fruit, and it has been sweet to your taste, and do you doubt Me? My left hand has been under your head, and My right hand has embraced you (Song 2:6). I have brought you to My banquet. I have feasted you with food such as angels have never tasted. I have filled your mouths with songs such as angels have never sung. I have promised you a heritage such as princes on earth might well envy, and do you doubt Me? Do you doubt Me, and do you doubt Me about such a matter as whether you will have food to eat and clothes to put on? Do the lilies doubt Me? Do the ravens doubt Me? And will you doubt Me about a matter concerning which lilies have no care, and the ravens have no thought? Do you doubt your eternal salvation when I have guaranteed to save you? Have I not sworn that I will surely deliver every soul who trusts in Me? What have I done to make you doubt Me like this? Where have I failed you? Show Me which promise I have broken, to which of My oaths I have been a traitor, or in what case I have turned My back on My friends. Oh, do not doubt Me!"

I wish that I could ask every doubter, *"How is it that ye have no faith?"* using the same tenderness that Jesus used. I think that if you could see His wounds, He would then say to you, "Can you distrust Me when I have these tokens of love in My hands, My feet, and My side? Can you doubt Me?" And as He asked the question, He would make you feel that it stirred an anguish in His soul, if it did not in yours. It was a painful question to the One who asked it.

An Important Question for Us to Hear

Unfortunately, it was necessary for the disciples to hear this question, and it is necessary for us to hear it, too. I would like to individualize a little, to hold the mirror up before you, my reader, so that you might see yourself.

There are some who are doubting Christ because they are in temporary trial. Perhaps you never were in such a sad position as you are in right now. Business seems to be going completely contrary to your designs. Your flood tide has suddenly ebbed, and your ship threatens to be left high and dry on a sandbar. You have a promise from God that this will not be, for He said, *"Trust in the LORD, and do good; so shalt thou dwell in the land, and verily thou shalt be fed"* (Ps. 37:3). He has said, *"Cast thy burden upon the LORD, and he shall sustain thee: he shall never suffer the righteous to be moved"* (Ps. 55:22). Yet, for all that, you cannot bravely look your trial in the face!

Perhaps there is a trouble coming tomorrow. Or, there is a season of trial coming in a week's time. You have taken it before God in prayer, yet even after you have prayed over it and asked for God's help, you have said to a friend, "I do not know how I will ever get through it." Now, was that right? Was that trusting your heavenly Friend? Has He not helped you before? Has He not delivered you from six troubles, even from seven (Job 5:19)? Will any evil touch you? Come, dear sister; come, dear brother; come at once to the mercy seat with your burdens. Oh, may God give you faith enough to tell your case before Him, and you will then hear Him say, *"As thy days, so shall thy strength be"* (Deut. 33:25).

Another person is reading this whose trouble is not about gold and silver, food and clothing. It is much worse; it is a trouble about his soul. He has lately been overwhelmed with a very terrible temptation, and wherever he goes it haunts him. He tries to run away from it, but he thinks he might as well try to run away from his own shadow. It clings to him. It seems to have fastened on his hand as the viper did upon Paul (Acts 28:3), and he cannot shake it off. He is afraid, indeed, that he will never be able to overcome this strong temptation. Read God's promise:

There hath no temptation taken you but such as is common to man: but God is faithful, who

will not suffer [allow] *you to be tempted above*
that ye are able; but will with the temptation
also make a way to escape, that ye may be able
to bear it.   *(1 Cor. 10:13)*

Then, *"how is it that ye have no faith?"* Did the
Lord Jesus not teach you to pray, *"Lead us not into*
temptation" (Matt. 6:13)? You have prayed that. Did
He not tell you to add, *"But deliver us from evil"* (v.
13), as though, if the first petition were not answered, the second one might be? You have prayed
this, and you believe that God hears prayer. How is
it, then, that you have no faith to believe that He
will hear you in this particular case? Beloved, Christ
is not a Savior for some things, but for all things. He
does not come in to help His people only on certain
days and only under certain assaults. He comes to
their rescue in all temptations and in all trials. Weak
as you are, He can strengthen you. Fierce though the
temptation may be, He can cover you from head to
foot with a full suit of armor in which you will stand
gloriously clothed.

The question *"How is it that ye have no faith?"*
might just as properly be asked of some Christians in
view of service that they might do for Christ. You do
not preach in the street, though you have the ability
to do so. You say you could never stand up to face the
crowd. *"How is it that ye have no faith?"* You do not
teach in the Sunday school. You sometimes think you
ought to try it, but you can hardly get enough courage. *"How is it that ye have no faith?"* You would like
to say a word or two to an ungodly friend, but you are
afraid that it would be of no use and that you would
be laughed at. *"How is it that ye have no faith?"*

Can you not say as Nehemiah did, *"Should such*
a man as I flee?" (Neh. 6:11). Who are you that you

should be afraid of a mortal man? Take courage, and do your Master's will. Has He not most certainly said, *"Fear not, thou worm Jacob, and ye men of Israel; I will help thee, saith the LORD, and thy redeemer, the Holy One of Israel"* (Isa. 41:14)? You know that these are His words. Then, *"how is it that ye have no faith?"* If we had more faith, dear friend, we would be doing a great deal more, and we would succeed in it. For lack of faith we do not try, and for lack of trying we do not perform. We are little nobodies when we might serve the Master and do much, if we only had more faith in Him.

There is another person reading this book who is afraid to die. He has been a Christian for many years, but whenever the thought of death crosses his mind, he tries to shake it off. He is a believer in Christ, but he is afraid that he will not be able to endure the last trying hour. I remember a sermon that my grandfather once preached that was rather unusual. His text was, *"The God of all grace"* (1 Pet. 5:10), and he finished each point by saying that God would give His people all grace. "But," he said at the close of each point, "there is one kind of grace you do not want." He gave this refrain several times: "There is one kind of grace you do not want." I think his hearers were all puzzled, but they received his message well enough when he closed by saying, "And the kind of grace that you do not want is dying grace in living moments, for you only want that when the time comes to die."

It may be that, as I am now, I could not bravely die. Yet, I am persuaded that the most timid woman, the most despondent man, if he or she is resting on Jesus, will be able to sing in death's tremendous hour! Do not be afraid, beloved! God will give you extraordinary courage when you come to extraordinary trial.

Like young Hopeful in *The Pilgrim's Progress,* when you cross the river of death, you will be able to say, "I feel the bottom, and it is good."

There is a good foothold through the river of death since Jesus Christ has died. Do not trouble yourself about dying if you have already died with Christ, for His word is sure: *"He that believeth in me, though he were dead, yet shall he live: and whosoever liveth and believeth in me shall never die"* (John 11:25–26). Take courage. If you are in bondage through fear of death, I ask you this question: *"How is it that ye have no faith?"*

Perhaps it will be best to conclude this list by saying that the question *"How is it that ye have no faith?"* might often meet us at our prayer closet doors. I hope all of us who profess to be believers in Christ know the power of prayer, for if we do not, we are fearful hypocrites. Perhaps you have been praying, but, beloved, is it not very possible that you leave your prayer closet doubting whether you have been heard? You have asked for a certain mercy, but you do not expect it, and the Lord might well say, *"How is it that ye have no faith?"* You often do not have the blessing because you do not believe that God will give you what you ask for.

However, remember that *"all things are possible to him that believeth"* (Mark 9:23). God denies nothing to a fervent heart when it can plead a promise and lay hold of Him by the hand of faith. I desire to have in all our churches a growing group of people who can pray! One of the Caesars had what he called "a thundering legion," and these were men who were Christians and could pray. The saying is true that the man who is mighty on his knees is mighty everywhere. If you can conquer God in prayer, you can certainly conquer your fellowman.

If, when wrestling with the angel as Jacob did, you can emerge the victor, you do not need to be afraid to wrestle with the very Devil himself, for you will be more than a match for him through the Lord Jesus Christ.

A Humbling Question for Us to Answer

"How is it that ye have no faith?" Dear friend, I think that this is a very humbling question for us to answer. I do not wish to answer it for you, but I want to propose it to every Christian so that he may answer it himself. But I do want to help you answer it.

Can you make a good excuse for your unbelief? I frankly confess that I cannot find any excuse for mine! I will tell you my history because I would not be surprised if it is very much like yours. I was a stranger to God and to hope. Jesus sought me. His Spirit taught me my need for Him, and I began to cry to Him. No sooner did I cry than He heard me, and at length He said to me, "Look, poor trembler, look to Me, and I will give you peace." I did look, and I had peace, a peace that I bless God I have never wholly lost these many years. I looked to Him and was radiant, and my face was not ashamed (Ps. 34:5).

Since then He has led me in a good path in His providence. My trials have not been as many as I deserve, but still enough. However, my strength has equaled my days (Deut. 33:25). In temporary matters, I have had an abundant supply; in spiritual matters, the fountain has never dried up. In my darkest nights, He has been my star; in my brightest days, He has been my sun. When my enemies have been too many for me, I have left them with Him, and He has routed them. When my burdens have been too heavy for me to carry, I have cast them upon Him. He has never seemed to make much of them but has carried them as some great creature might carry a grain of sand. I do not have a word to say against Him.

If He continues to act toward me as He has done, and if I could live to be as old as the martyr Polycarp and were asked to curse Him, I would have to answer as he did, "How can I curse Him? What have I to say against Him?" He has never broken His promise; He has never failed in His Word. He has been to me the best Master that a man ever had, though I have been one of the worst of His servants. He has been true and faithful to every "jot and tittle," blessed be His name. If He were to say to me, *"How is it that ye have no faith?"* I am sure I do not know what I could answer. I could only hide my face and say, "My Master, I seem to be almost a devil to think that I cannot believe more firmly in such a one as You are—so good, so true, so kind." No, I cannot make an excuse for myself, and I do not suppose that you can make an excuse for yourself.

I suppose, however, that the real reason for our lack of faith lies in this, that we have low thoughts of God compared with the thoughts that we ought to have. We do not think that He is as mighty, as good, and as tender as He is. Then, again, we have very leaky memories. We forget His mighty arm. We forget what He did in days past. Mount Hermon (Deut. 3:8) and Mizar Hill (Ps. 42:6) we pass by, and we let His loving-kindness be forgotten.

I am afraid, too, that we rely too much on ourselves. Was it not Dr. Gordon who, when he lay dying, said that the secret of having strong faith in Christ is having no faith in ourselves? I am inclined to think that the reason we have weak faith in God is that we have a good deal of self-reliance. But, when you cannot trust in yourself, then you hang onto Christ and cling to Him as your only hope. Then you have the grip of a sinking man, and there is no hold like that. There is no hold like the hold of someone who says, "If I do not grip this, there is nothing else in all the world."

> Other refuge have I none,
> Hangs my helpless soul on Thee.

I am afraid it is our self-confidence that comes in to mar our trust in God. And, besides that, there is our *"evil heart of unbelief, in departing from the living God"* (Heb. 3:12). I said the other day, concerning some sad, sad temptation into which a brother had fallen, that I wished the Devil were dead. But after a while I corrected myself and said that I wished that I were dead myself, for if my own self were dead and gone, and Christ lived in me, I would not mind the Devil. But when the Devil and my own self get together, they make a sorry mess of things. His sparks would be harmless if I did not have any kindling, but it is the kindling in me that does the mischief. He might try his hardest to break into my house, but if my house were not a poor clay tenement, he would never be able to get in. Oh, Lord Jesus, come and live in my heart! Fill it with Yourself, and then there can be no room for Satan. Do keep me even unto the end.

With this I conclude what I have to say to those of you who are Christians. I only beg to say to every doubting Christian, *"How is it that ye have no faith?"* Give a good account for your lack of faith, if you can. I have never heard a good excuse made for that wicked sinner, Mr. Nobelief. He cannot be put to death for some reason, but I often wish that he could be blown to pieces from the muzzles of the guns of God's promises. Oh, that the last rag and the last remnant of him were completely destroyed! John Bunyan, in *The Holy War,* portrayed the citizens of Mansoul going around to pick up the bones of the traitors and burying them all, until, he said, "There was not the least bone, or rag, or piece of a bone of a traitor left." Oh, I wish we could get to that state—that there were not the least bone, rag, or piece of a bone of a doubter left, so that we might sing confidently concerning our God.

Those Who Are Non-Christians

Now, solemnly and most affectionately, I want to write to those who have never believed in Christ.

To some of you, Christ's head crowned with thorns is no object of reverence. You have never looked up to the Man of Sorrows and felt that *"surely he hath borne our griefs, and carried our sorrows"* (Isa. 53:4). It is nothing to you that Jesus had to die. Up to this moment, you have been a stranger to Him. Now, I beg to ask you the question, *"How is it that ye have no faith?"* This question is not an impertinent one, but a very natural one. Allow me to help you by applying this question to you.

Faith Makes the Christian Happy

Do you not know that faith makes the Christian happy? There are Christians with very small incomes—a few dollars a week. They are living in the depths of poverty, yet they would not trade places with kings. They are very happy because faith makes them rich. There are others who have an abundance of this world's goods, yet they can truly say that they would give them all up if God so willed it, for material things are not their gods. Our springs of joy come from Christ. Faith makes men happy.

"How is it that ye have no faith?" You squander your substance to get a day's amusement. Do you *"spend money for that which is not bread? and your labour for that which satisfieth not"* (Isa. 55:2)? Here is something that is bread, that would satisfy you. Why do you not have it? You working men, you sons of toil, possessing little to make you happy, *"how is it that ye have no faith?"* Faith would make your cottage as blessed as a palace, and a scanty loaf to be better than a fattened calf.

Faith Sustains the Christian in Death

You know, too, that it is faith that enables the Christian to die well. You expect to die soon, too. You must soon depart. *"How is it that ye have no faith?"* You are like the man who has to cross a river but has made no provision for it, or who is going on a long journey but takes no money with him. How is it that you have nothing to help you die? It is faith that conducts the Christian to heaven. We sing of the realms of the blessed and of Canaan's happy land, but faith is the only passport to the skies. Therefore, *"how is it that ye have no faith?"* Do you not desire a blessed future? Do you have no wish for immortal joys? Does your heart never leap at the thought of the joys that the saints have before the throne? How is it that you let these things slip by, having no faith? *"Without faith it is impossible to please* [God]" (Heb. 11:6), and the faithless will have their portion in the lake that burns with fire (Rev. 21:8).

"How is it that ye have no faith?" Do you intend to venture into that state of misery? Do you intend to challenge the Day of Judgment without an Advocate and a Friend? You will have to rise again. Though the worms destroy your body, in your flesh you will have to see God (Job 19:26). The trumpet will be sounding, the angels will be gathering, the judgment seat will be set, and you will be called to account. Without faith, you will be driven from His presence into black despair. Then, *"how is it that ye have no faith?"* When I think about these things, it does seem strange to me that men should be living in utter indifference to Christ and in neglect of divine things! *"How is it?"*—can anyone tell us—*"How is it that ye have no faith?"*

Faith Is Not a Difficult Thing

Are there difficult things that you cannot understand? Now, what is it that you are asked to believe? Simply this, that sin is so evil and bitter a thing that God must punish it, and that His own dear Son became a man and suffered for our sins. Those sins may be readily pardoned for all those who trust Him, because Christ suffered the punishment of them. Really, that does not strike me as being a very difficult thing to believe. To trust my soul with the Son of God, bleeding and dying upon Calvary, does not strike me as being in itself a very difficult thing. If it is difficult, it surely must be the hardness of our hearts that makes it so. There is no doctrine under heaven that is more reasonable, that more deserves to be received than this, that Jesus Christ came into the world to save sinners, even the worst (1 Tim. 1:15).

I do not think that when you are asked why you have no faith, you can reply that it is because you do

204

not know what you have to believe. I know that I have tried to make it plain enough. If I knew of any words in the English language that would be plainer than any I have used, even if they were so down-to-earth that I would be criticized by everyone for using them, I would use them if I thought I could win one soul by them. The simple truth is that whoever trusts Christ is saved, and I have tried to explain this thoroughly, so that lack of knowledge is not the reason that you have no faith.

Faith Requires Thought

I am afraid that in many cases lack of faith is from a lack of thought. Oh, many people are mere butterflies! They think about their work or about their pleasures, but not about their souls. It is not always a bad sign when a person begins to be skeptical. I would sooner have him skeptical than thoughtless, for even to think about spiritual things is good. Men are often like certain bats that cannot take off from the ground; they must get on a stone, and then, when they are elevated a little, they can move their wings. In the same way, thoughtless men are on the ground and cannot fly, but when God gets them thinking, they seem as if they are moving their wings.

I encourage you to think about spiritual matters, for certainly it must be recognized by every reasonable person that the eternal part of man ought to be the part most thought of. This poor, mortal rag, which will drop into the grave, should not command my highest and most continuous thought. But the immortal principle within me, which will outlive the stars and be a thing of life and vigor when the sun has shut its burning eye from

205

dim old age—this immortal part of my nature certainly ought to have my most serious and my best thought. If you are obliged to say that you have no faith because you have not thought much about it, I pray that you will think. May God help you so that this thinking leads you to faith.

Faith Can Be Yours

But, to close, the question I have asked you is a question that I hope you will never be asked anymore. May this be the last time that anyone has to ask you, *"How is it that ye have no faith?"* In order to make this wish true, however, you must believe now. To believe is to trust Christ Jesus. The Son of the everlasting God took upon Himself the form of man and suffered, and He tells us that if we rest on Him, He will be better to us than our faith. There has never been a man who trusted in Christ and found Him a liar. If you trust Christ, you will be saved; no, you are saved. And the proof of your being saved will be this, that you will not be the same person any longer. All things will become new with you (2 Cor. 5:17). You will be saved from sinning as well as from the guilt of sin. The alcoholic will become sober. The dishonest will become pure. The mere moralist will become spiritual. The enemy of God will become His friend.

> Loved of my God, for Him again
> With love intense I burn.

I cannot help but love Him who has saved me from my sins.

May God bless this question to you, but if it has not been of use to you yet, I hope that it will follow you. I would like to pin it to your back, but it would be better if I could pin it to your heart. I hope that it will wake you up at night. I trust it will be with you at breakfast tomorrow. Between the intervals of business, I hope that there will come a voice from under the counter, or from the back of the work-shop, *"How is it that ye have no faith?"* And in the evening, when you walk alone on the streets awhile, may it be almost as though someone had touched you on the shoulder and said, *"How is it that ye have no faith?"*

I assure you that if this question does not haunt you now, one day it will. The day will come when, stretched out on a lonely bed, you must bid the world good-bye. Then there may seem to be before you the ghastly form of Death, who, with bony finger uplifted, will preach a sermon to you that your very heart and your very bones will feel. He will say to you, "How is it? *'How is it that ye have no faith?'"*

Oh, may you never be asked that question again. May you now believe in the Lord Jesus Christ and be saved!